PRAISE FOR

Jeff Mock's *You Can Write Poetry*

"*You Can Write Poetry* is a fresh, lively guide that will be equally valuable to aspiring poets, readers and teachers of poetry. Mock covers the basics with clarity and engaging warmth, showing how all aspects of the craft are related. I especially like his use of 'practice sessions' because he keeps our attention where it should be—on the process rather than on the products (the poems). Through anecdotes, examples and plain talk, Mock offers numerous points of entry into a difficult art. Relaxed and conversational in style, this is nevertheless an ambitious and accomplished book."
   —Chase Twichell, poet and author of *The Practice of Writing Poetry*

"Jeff Mock has issued an open invitation to the beginning poet, one that's practical without getting pedestrian, and inspiring without getting blurry-eyed. He escorts the novice safely beyond the popular fallacies that writing poetry requires a Ph.D. in literature and a current license from the Academy of American Poets or, at the other extreme, that it requires nothing more than an inclination to unplug the rational/critical faculties and scrawl down whatever surfaces. The emphasis is on steady work and craftsmanship, but not at the exclusion of imagination and fun. Mock also stresses reading and studying good poetry as he does—regularly and lovingly. The beginner can go to this book for friendly instruction and advice, the non-beginner for a fresh, concise review of the fundamentals. My students would love this book."
   —William Trowbridge, author of *Enter Dark Stranger* and *O Paradise*

"With its friendly explanations, inspiring examples, and downright fun exercises, Mock's book is sure to convince the beginning writer just what the title promises: *You Can Write Poetry*."
   —Robin Behn, author of *Paper Bird*

"To paraphrase Emily Dickinson, I'll tell you how this book rises: one brick at a time. Poetry is the house, and Jeff Mock builds it soundly and imaginatively. First, he lays the foundation—showing us the importance of reading poetry, establishing regular writing habits, and choosing the most evocative words. He moves on to furnishings, the concrete and specific details that make a house a home, creating rooms that echo with memory and delight. Finally, windows open to gardens—formal and informal, wild and tame. As we leave the premises, we feel fortunate to have been given such a personal and thorough tour. Viewing Mock's house of poetry from the inside out, we are emboldened to try our hand—yes, why not? Pick up a hammer and begin."

— Rebecca McClanahan, author of *The Intersection of X and Y*, *Mrs. Houdini* and *Mother Tongue*

You Can Write Poetry

JEFF MOCK

WRITER'S DIGEST BOOKS
CINCINNATI, OHIO

Other fine Writer's Digest Books are available from your local bookstore or direct from the publisher.

02 01 00 99 98   5 4 3 2 1

Library of Congress Cataloging-in-Publication Data

Mock, Jeff.
  You can write poetry / by Jeff Mock.—1st ed.
      p.   cm.
  Includes index.
  ISBN 0-89879-825-6 (pbk. : alk. paper)
  1. Poetry—Authorship. 2. Creative writing. I. Title.
PN1059.A9M63   1998
808.1—dc21   98-12073
                                                     CIP

Editors: Jack Heffron and Chantelle Bentley
Production Editor: Nicole R. Klungle
Cover designers: Brian Roeth and Mary Barnes Clark
Designers: Sandy Conopeotis Kent and Mary Barnes Clark

PERMISSIONS

"Pale Spring" by Ian Clarke is reprinted by permission of the author. Originally appeared in *The Laurel Review*.

"My Father as Houdini" by Mark Drew is reprinted by permission of the author. Originally appeared in *The Gettysburg Review*.

"Building a New Home" by Tim Geiger is reprinted by permission of the author. Originally appeared in *Defined Providence*.

"We Grow Accustomed to the Dark" by Kathleen Halme is reprinted by permission of the author. Originally appeared in *The Gettysburg Review*.

"When" by Katherine Riegel is reprinted by permission of the author. Originally appeared in *The River King Poetry Supplement*.

"The Waking" by Theodore Roethke is reprinted by permission of Doubleday, a division of Bantam Doubleday Dell Publishing Group, Inc. Originally appeared in *The Collected Poems of Theodore Roethke*.

"One Sunday Each Spring" by Margot Schilpp is reprinted by permission of the author. Originally appeared in *Connecticut Review*.

ACKNOWLEDGMENTS

Thanks go to Cinda Gibbon for reading the manuscript-in-progress, making corrections and offering sage advice; to Peter Stitt for letting me out of the office and giving me time to write; to Jack Heffron for suggesting this book and running the show; and to Joan, wife and friend, for her inspiration and encouragement.

ABOUT THE AUTHOR

Jeff Mock is a professor of creative writing at Southern Connecticut State University and the author of *Evening Travelers*, a limited-edition, fine-press chapbook. Formerly an editor of *The Gettysburg Review*, he has published poems in *The Chicago Review*, *The Laurel Review* and *New England Review*, among several others. He has received the *Greensboro Review* Literary Award in Poetry, a Teaching-Writing Fellowship at the University of Alabama and a scholarship to the Bread Loaf Writer's Conference.

TABLE OF CONTENTS

1 WHY WRITE?

Toward the end of autumn, early on a Saturday so sunny and blue that you can see for miles through the crystal air, my wife Joan wakes and puts on her dirt-digging clothes: an old sweatshirt, baggy jeans and sneakers that have seen better days. She dons a pair of sturdy work gloves, grabs a trowel and out the door she goes to plant bulbs on one of the season's last perfect days. Crocus, muscari, tulip, daffodil and hyacinth—she digs, fertilizes, sets them in and covers them up. She plants a hundred bulbs or more, digging earth up and patting it down. A few weeks later, the northern wind blows in with its quick freeze. Snow follows. Throughout the winter, she waits, cultivating patience. The days are short, the nights are long, and the snow piles up.

Then the days lengthen. The weather turns, the snow begins its slow melt, and spring arrives. Joan dons her dirt-digging clothes again and goes out to plant the year's annuals—petunia, moss rose, geranium and salvia. She plants perennials, too—cornflower, red-hot poker, fox-glove, delphinium and her favorite lilies, daylily, Asiatic and trumpet. It takes time. Our soil is rugged, rock and clay making for rough digging. And we have eight flower beds on our small lot—eight so far, that is. It takes much of a Saturday and a Sunday, and the following weekend, and the weekend following that. But the rewards are worth the effort. From March through October, Joan's flower beds burst and dazzle. They flare with hues across the spectrum, the vibrant and subtle alike.

I can barely water houseplants, but gardening is one of Joan's talents, and perhaps a gift. She takes her gardening seriously, too, although you'd wonder. She receives so much pleasure from planting and tending her flowers that her efforts don't seem much like labor. Her labor and her pleasure are married in her achievements. I step outside—front door, side or back, it doesn't matter—and see our yard in bloom, and I know that Joan has made an art of gardening.

That's the key: making art of what you do.

Joan's mother gardens, too, and Joan's youngest brother is an organic farmer. My mother practices arts and crafts, and my eldest sister is a professional painter who restores old Victorian homes to their original glory. It amazes me that all of these people are, in their own ways, artists. But it shouldn't amaze me. Creativity finds ways to express itself. It happens every day. My neighbors are artists, too: chefs and mechanics, teachers and preachers, dentists and woodworkers. They all create, fashion and make art of what they do. The urge to create spurs us on. The ways to express it are varied and numerous.

Poetry is the way I've chosen, or perhaps poetry chose me. I suspect the latter. I began writing poetry in my early teens. I didn't know it then, but poetry was helping me think through the conflicting emotions that accompany growing up. It helped me survive my first full-blown, ill-fated romance. Later, poetry even helped me marry Joan. Now I write to think through the conflicting emotions that come from having grown up. Poetry, like life, is an ongoing process.

Against my mother's advice, I studied literature in college—but only after trying economics, business, accounting, journalism and several other "sensible" areas of study. Through all of my educational misadventures, I found myself making time to write poems, an evening here, a morning there. I wrote poems—and read them—because I felt compelled to. Mostly I wrote bad poems, a great many bad poems, but that was very much a part of learning to write better poems. I studied poetry; I read poems every day. I wrote bad poems and then better poems. I studied more. I wrote more.

Since then, I've taught poetry writing to students in elementary, junior high and high schools, and in the university. I also spent seven years as an editor with a literary magazine, *The Gettysburg Review*. Even if all that weren't so, I'd still be writing and reading poems. I stare at a blank sheet of paper, wrack my brain and, finally, put words on the page. Sometimes, after much scribbling and crossing out and scribbling again, the words become a poem. Sometimes they don't. Regardless, I'm back at it the next day. There's something inside that insists on getting out. It's a thought, a pang, an elation, a question. It gets into me. It rattles around. It navigates the pathways between my head and heart. It poses a *what if?* It asks *what then?*

Why write? Because you feel this drive, impulse, force, passion. Because you think, feel, imagine and are compelled to craft the language, thus giving form to thought, emotion and imagination. William Shakespeare describes the passion in his play *A Midsummer Night's Dream*:

> The poet's eye, in a fine frenzy rolling,
> Doth glance from heaven to earth, from earth to heaven;
> And as imagination bodies forth
> The forms of things unknown, the poet's pen
> Turns them to shapes, and gives to airy nothing
> A local habitation and a name.

You feel it, too, the urge to imagine and invent, to put words on the page, to make poems. Because this urge has *you*, welcome. Welcome to poetry.

What to Expect

You may wonder if there's a sensible way of writing poems. Yes—and no. By that, I mean it depends. Samuel Johnson, the eighteenth-century English writer and critic, said, "Poetry is the art of uniting pleasure with truth, by calling imagination to the help of reason." On the one hand you have imagination, and on the other you have reason. Poetry is an odd combination of the two, and they don't go easily together, which means there's no sure-shot, 1-2-3 system for writing poems. But whether the making of poems is sensible or not, yes, you can learn to write poems.

What distinguishes one kind of creativity, one art from another is knowledge of the subject. Well, knowledge and practice. Poetry takes a lot of practice. Even established poets practice to hone their skills. But practice is not always work; sometimes it's play. Work and play are both valuable, and both lead to good poems.

That's where this book comes in. It's designed for those who feel the urge to write poetry, but haven't had the formal training and practical experience. This book will provide a bit of both. In that sense, it will also benefit those who are already writing poems and wish to revisit their early lessons in the craft. It's a place to begin, or begin again.

Remember that this is a beginning, a jumping-off spot. There will always be more to learn, just as there will always be more poems to write. There's more to poetry than any one book can contain or any one teacher can teach. But this beginning will help you on your way to writing poems you can take pride in, poems that make your readers think and feel.

For my part, I'll offer practical advice. And because poetry isn't a wholly practical endeavor, I'll offer impractical advice, too. The *craft* of poetry, its rhythms and rhymes, has much to do with the practical. You can acquire the craft of poetry. You can learn about **similes** and **metaphors** (we'll cover those **figures of speech** in chapter six). You can learn to dance along an **iambic pentameter** line and to vary it on occasion by stepping into a **trochee** (chapter six). You can learn the intricacies of **rhyme schemes** and **sonnets** (chapter eight).

These topics appear in an order that will allow you to develop your skills and build on them. We begin with the nature of words themselves, go on to such aspects of poetry as figures of speech, rhyme and meter, and come out with poetic forms and free verse. While I discuss these aspects one at a time, they don't work their magic one at a time. They're all in play simultaneously. Poems are busy places.

Practice will help you write better poems. Throughout this book, you'll find practice sessions to engage you and hone your skills. Take your time with the sessions. Some even call for several days of writing. Don't think of these writings as finished poems, but as starting places. They're drafts of poems-to-be. Keep them together in a folder or write them in the pages of a notebook. You'll be generating words, ideas and emotions that may blossom into poems later. Feel free to repeat any (or perhaps all) of these exercises. Add to them if you like. To be a poet, you need to write; these practice sessions will get you going.

I'll also present poems for you to read, some old and some new, and recommend other poems and poets for you to read. You can learn a great deal about writing from reading poems. I encourage you to read deeply and widely, because in addition to its pleasure, reading is a way to see what can be done with words. Poems I've read in various books and literary magazines have been among my best teachers. I read and learn from them. When I'm ready to learn more, I read them again.

Here, for example, is a poem I admire and read several times a year, a poem of loneliness and love, written around 1530 by an unknown poet:

WESTERN WIND

Western wind, when wilt thou blow,
The small rain down can rain?
Christ, if my love were in my arms,
And I in my bed again!

This is an old poem and its syntax is slightly different from what you're used to. Read the second line as "so that the small rain down can rain." The **speaker** of the poem (in this case a first-person speaker, the *I*) asks the wind to blow in a storm so the sky will release its rain and, in a sense, cry. The drops of rain become tears, a further expression of the speaker's loneliness. (This is an instance of **imagery**, which we'll cover in chapter four.) "Western Wind" is a simple poem, and its emotional power resides precisely in its simplicity, in its direct statement of desire: "Christ, if my love were in my arms, / And I in my bed again!" One thing "Western Wind" has taught me is that while poems often work subtly, through implication, an artfully rendered direct statement can provide or intensify a poem's intellectual and emotional power.

We'll also look into some of the intangibles of poetry: whimsy, sounds and echoes, sense and nonsense, poetic questioning. The *art* of poetry is more than the *craft* of poetry. The art of poetry depends on the poet's ability to see and hear clearly what others do not, to say precisely what others haven't the language to say themselves—sometimes offering answers, always posing questions. These intangibles are the impractical and absolutely necessary aspects of poetry. They're part of the curiosity and questing intelligence of the poet.

It's better to have more questions than answers, because poetry thrives on the uncertain. It savors exploration. It lives on discovery. Poets rarely write because they know what they want to say. Rather, they write to discover the words that must be said. If you do this, if you set out to explore, you'll discover the words you have to say. In that discovery, you'll create poems. With practice, much writing and revision, you'll create the poems that only you can. As a poet, you have a responsibility, to yourself and to the readers of your poems, to make each poem as good as it can be.

Revision, the spit and polish of poetry, is the process through which you make art of your first writings.

But that comes later. We're at the beginning now. There's more to come: knowledge and practice, reading and writing, the poems you have in you now and those that will follow. Exploration beckons. Discoveries await. Welcome to this grand adventure. Again, welcome to poetry.

PRACTICE SESSION

1. Describe a photograph, preferably an old photograph. Describe what appears within the framed scene. Describe the day the photo was taken. Describe what's just outside the framed scene. Describe what the photographer was thinking. What did the photographer want to preserve by taking this photograph?

2. Write down a dream. Don't try to make sense of it. Instead, describe it in as much detail as you can. What aspects of the dream are most vivid? What aspects interest you most?

3. Explain why the chicken crossed the road. What did it leave? What did it cross to? What was the chicken thinking? Did it have ulterior motives for crossing the road? What other factors contributed to the chicken's decision? Make up the rationales as you go.

4. Write without pause for ten minutes, beginning with the phrase *It was the best. . . .* Don't pause to think about what to write. Don't worry about making sense. Write as quickly as you can. Write everything that comes to mind.

5. Select five words at random from a dictionary. Write a draft of a poem using all five words. Include a kangaroo in the draft. Remember, don't think of this writing as a poem; it's a draft, a place to start. Later, you may decide to return to it. For now, just write.

2 SHARPENING THE PENCIL

When I was a student, the university brought in established poets several times a year to read their poems and talk with students about writing. We asked about the process of writing. We wanted to know what exactly a poem is, where the poets wrote, with pencil or pen? Whether they wrote in the morning or evening—every day? Where did they find their subjects? What did they do to become poets? What does it take? The responses to these questions were similar from poet to poet. Different poets keep different habits, but the process of writing is basically the same. Poets become poets by writing poems.

What a Poem Is

Robert Frost, the quintessential American poet, said that a poem "begins in delight and ends in wisdom." That isn't a practical description of poetry, but then poetry isn't a wholly practical endeavor. Frost's definition is the truest I know. If a poem doesn't delight its reader, if it doesn't inspire an *oh* or an *ah*, the reader sets it aside and it collects dust. If the reader isn't in some way wiser for and enriched by reading a poem, the poem has been mere entertainment. For that we have television, movies, music, comic strips and numerous other pastimes. (But, of course, poems do entertain, too.)

So what is a poem? It's something that needs to be said, and said in a way that captures the reader's attention.

A poem expresses an idea, emotion, experience or all three. It tells a story. It portrays a character. It describes a scene. It sings a song. It relates a conflict. It meditates on a walk through the woods, late in the afternoon of a brisk autumn day, as maple and oak leaves come loose in the wind and twirl down into the rustling brush. A poem does any of these, all of these, or something completely different. The question is, what does the poet want the poem to do? Or, rather, what does the poem want the poet to do? Poems work that way; they take off on their own, and the poet has to keep up with them.

Mainly, a poem is an artistic expression of the imagination that takes place in language. Even when it relates an actual event—waking to birdsong, cooking lunch, gardening or changing the oil in your car—a poem is always an artistic expression created in words. The language is more important than the event it relates. It is the medium of the art. Words are the bricks that build the house; just as a house is built brick by brick, a poem is built word by word. So even when writing a poem about an actual event, the poet filters the event through imagination and re-creates it in words. The event does not make the poem; language makes the poem, and imagination crafts the language. In essence, the poet *translates* the event into language, and the reader experiences the translation as an event-in-words. Through study and practice, the poet learns to craft the language so any event, even the most mundane, takes on a new life. It becomes an event worth experiencing through the art of poetry.

Poems are imagined onto the page, one word after another. The poet selects words for their economy and resonance. Each word must be the best possible word—a word that is absolutely necessary (economy) and echoes with meaning (resonance). (A great many words in English have more than one meaning, and poets often select such words to use their multiple meanings.) A poem, then, is imagination put concisely and precisely into the most expressive language. The poet uses imagery, metaphor, sound and rhythm (more on these in chapters four and six), and these aspects of poetry work together.

The defining characteristic of poetry, as opposed to prose, is that poetry is written in lines. *Verse* is another term for poetry. It comes from the Latin *versus*, which means "a turning." A line of poetry doesn't stretch completely across the page. It *turns* back before reaching the right-hand margin, and another line begins. Then again, some poems have lines longer than the width of the page. Unlike prose, poetry doesn't depend on the right-hand margin to determine the length of its lines. As with the poet's selection of words, the placement of this **line break** is important. You'll read more about line breaks in chapters six and eight, but for now, as you read poems, notice the line breaks. Consider why the poet chose to turn the line there. Does the line break stop you for a moment with punctuation (an **end-stopped line**)? Or does the line turn in midphrase and lead you quickly on to the next line (an **enjambed line**)?

Like other specialized fields, poetry has its own terminology, its own lingo, that describes the various aspects of a poem. If a carpenter calls for a saber saw, for example, he doesn't want a reciprocating saw, circular saw or band saw. If a doctor talks about a tibia, she doesn't mean a fibula, femur or patella. The terms may seem troublesome at first, but poets use these terms to speak to each other precisely and effectively about poetry. It's also simpler and more direct to say *line break* instead of *the place where the line turns.*

My students in Introduction to Literature courses often thought of poems as puzzles to be figured out. This common misunderstanding results from the very nature of poetry, which is meant to be rich with meaning. With a good poem, you notice something new each time you read it, just as you notice something new each time you view a painting, watch a film or listen to music. Reading a poem for the second, fifth or twentieth time, you notice a certain nuance, perceive a verb's double meaning or hear the repetition of certain sounds. You see (and hear) the poem's intricacies. The poem may be subtle and complex. It means what it says and says what it means.

So how should you begin? If you enlisted in the navy and didn't know how to swim, the navy used to have a simple lesson (perhaps it still does): Heave ho, overboard you go. Sink or swim. Learning what a poem is, and learning how to write poems, is similar. Jump in. Immerse yourself. Float, dog-paddle and then swim. The more you're in the water, the better you swim. The better you swim, the more you're in the water. With poetry begin, say, by reading Shakespeare:

SONNET 18

Shall I compare thee to a summer's day?
Thou art more lovely and more temperate:
Rough winds do shake the darling buds of May,

And summer's lease hath all too short a date;
Sometime too hot the eye of heaven shines,
And often is his gold complexion dimm'd;
And every fair from fair sometime declines,
By chance or nature's changing course untrimm'd:
But thy eternal summer shall not fade
Nor lose possession of that fair thou ow'st;
Nor shall Death brag thou wand'rest in his shade,
When in eternal lines to time thou grow'st;
So long as men can breathe or eyes can see,
So long lives this, and this gives life to thee.

This is a poem of complex metaphors, yet it's clear enough. The speaker compares someone, the *thee*, favorably to a summer day. As summer turns to autumn, that someone also ages and pales, but the speaker goes on to say in the final line that as long as *this*, the poem, survives, that someone also survives. In lauding that person's beauty, the poem keeps that person alive.

Reading poetry helps you understand for yourself what poetry is. What do you like? What do you dislike? Read Shakespeare, his poems and plays. Read poems by John Keats and William Butler Yeats, Percy Bysshe Shelley and Emily Dickinson, Robert Frost and William Carlos Williams. Because you want to write good poems, aspire to write as well as Shakespeare and these other masters. Decide that you'll make each of your poems as perfect as you can. Set your standards high and don't settle for less. It requires much practice and play, but your poems will be only as good as you expect them to be. Expect much from them.

 PRACTICE
SESSION

1. Read five poems you've never read before. Write down what you like and dislike about each poem. Summarize them: What are their subjects, and what do they say about those subjects?

2. Repeat exercise one with five poems you love. Compare your notes. What similarities and differences do you see?

The Poet's Discipline

Writing poems comes easily some days, but not most. It requires discipline. If you've had a pet, you already know about discipline. The same rule for having a pet applies to writing: Take responsibility. If you want the company of a dog—a mutt, say, a shepherd-terrier-and-who-knows-what-else mix named Woodrow—that means you have a responsibility. Joan and I have lived with Woodrow for seven years. It's been work. We lug home forty-pound bags of dog food. We romp with him, and tussle, and take him to the park so he can run off his energy. We groom him. Before bed, we take him around the block and clean up after him as we go. The evening walk is now a habit. In the heavy heat of summer, in the freezing bite of winter, round the block we go, every night, Woodrow leading the way. Has he been worth the work? Definitely. With the responsibility comes the pleasure of having a faithful, loving companion.

If you want the pleasures of writing poems, you have certain responsibilities. They're only slightly different from those of having a pet. You must feed your imagination by reading poems and by looking at and listening to the world around you. You must allow your imagination room to play, to take off and run. You must groom your poems regularly, which means revising them. You must be willing to throw out the bad writing. This last responsibility is difficult, but not everything you write will be good enough to keep. The same is true for every writer. No one writes well all the time. No one. The late poet and teacher William Stafford said, "A writer must write bad poems, as they come, among the better, and not scorn the 'bad' ones. Finicky ways can dry up the sources." He's absolutely right. The good poems will come. So will the bad. Don't fret about it. Learn to recognize the difference between the good and bad, but don't regret the bad poems. It's all part of writing.

As a poet, you have one primary responsibility: to write. Write every day. Make time if you must. Mornings, afternoons, evenings, it doesn't matter when, but set aside time every day to write. I do mean *every day*, even if for only a short while. You'll find the responsibility becoming habit, like walking Woodrow around the block. After the habit sets in, you'll find that you *need* to write. Every now and then, Joan sends me to my writing room. I've become surly. I snap at her for leaving the orange juice on the counter. I complain there's nothing to do. "Go," she says, "you need to write. Get to it." The urge to write is pushing at me and I am ignoring it, but Joan knows me well. So off I go to take care of what needs to be done. I start in on a new poem or dig out an old

11

draft that isn't working yet. I write. In a while, I feel better.

The responsibility becomes habit, and habit produces poems. If you don't write, you don't write poems. If you do write, the poems come. That's the reward and the satisfaction. That's the achievement. There's no pleasure like that of writing a good poem. And the more you write, the nearer you draw to the source of your poems, your wellspring, where the ideas and emotions gather and wait to be released.

Where Poems Come From

Sometimes inspiration visits you. The seed of a poem, the kernel of an idea, comes to you. It's a flash, the lightbulb snapping on above your head, the lightning bolt of an idea striking you. But inspiration isn't the poem. It's the beginning of the poem. Writing poems is similar to Joan's planting and tending her flower beds. The poet grasps the seed of a poem and plants it on the page. In time, the flowers and poems come up. They sprout, bud and bloom. That flash of inspiration still requires the poet's dedication to work on the poem.

If you feel inspired, you needn't worry about where poems come from. On the other hand, you must often take your cue from Thomas Edison: "Genius is 1 percent inspiration and 99 percent perspiration." Most of the time, poets must work to get on with the daily business, searching for ideas and the words to express them. So what do you do, then, to come up with ideas for poems?

One way—I think the best—is to keep a journal. Any notebook will do. Select one that fits your personality, one that you like to hold, one that invites you to fill it with words. Write what you see and hear, your dreams and daydreams, anything that crosses your mind, anything that strikes you as you read, anything that interests you. Actually, write everything that interests you, because these are the seeds of your poems. Your concerns become your poems. Take notes on poems you read. Comment on them. Argue with them if you disagree. Write lines or entire poems that take your breath away. Write interesting words, words you've recently learned, words that just sound good. Write anything that catches your eye, a tattered sheet of newsprint blown down the street or a couple of girls playing basketball in the park. Write a vivid dream in all its irrational detail. Write an errant thought, one that presents itself unexpectedly. Write down your involvement with the world.

Keep a journal so you can return to it later to spark ideas and invent poems. That's what many writers do. Because I have a spotty memory,

I write down as much as I can: ideas, sights, lines of poems, possible titles, strange words, words of advice, words of wisdom. Here are a few of the numerous notes in my journals:

- "A Short History of a Long Night" (a possible title)
- "The poet does not *use* poetry, but is at the service of poetry." (advice from an essay, "The Poet in the World," by Denise Levertov)
- "If you want to get a sure crop with a big yield, sow wild oats." (from a fortune cookie, honest)
- "North is pure delusion, snowblind and rapturous" (a line from a poem, "Diorama Notebook," by Kathleen Halme)
- "Kiss, kisser, kissing bug, kissing cousin, kissy, kissy-face" (dictionary entries)
- "Poem about a man who empties his pockets in a bar and tells tales of all the objects" (a stray thought)
- "Queen Mab: English folklore, a fairy queen who controls people's dreams" (another dictionary entry)
- "Boys from up the street with their snowshovels, one green shovel and one red" (the morning after a heavy snowfall)
- "The fact is the sweetest dream that labor knows." (a line from a poem, "Mowing," by Robert Frost)

My journals are idea logs, diaries of the imagination. I note whatever interests me and return to them later to gather ideas for poems.

One evening in Tuscaloosa, Alabama, I read this piece of graffiti, scrawled in green ink on the wall of a restroom in a blues pub: "I feel more like I did when I came in here than I do now." I loved it because it didn't make sense; it's a **paradox**, a contradiction that contains a grain of truth. It made my mind race, trying to figure it out. I wrote it down on a cocktail napkin and stuffed it into my pocket. That night when I returned home, I added it to my journal. A month or two later, I returned to it and began mulling it over. It started a poem brewing. Then it became the title of the poem, one of the earliest of mine to be published in a literary magazine:

I FEEL MORE LIKE I DID
WHEN I CAME IN HERE THAN I DO NOW

Sure, all roads lead round again to the heart,
But I'm lost in some far province—a toe

Or finger, peninsula—alone, hurt,
Sincere, and inconsequential. Each moment

I wake to strange sunrises, jollity
In a foreign tongue, air that smells of fish
And oil, grinding of sphinxian machinery
Down by the shore. There are no roads in this

Terra incognita. No petrol stations
To inquire directions. No maps for sale.
No rocks singing out advice. When I come
Upon starfish, they point five ways. Wee snails

Lumber down the beach, inch-by-inching outward.
The ocean rears up and back, gone and going.
Up in the hills, campfires blaze and the stars
Snap on. I hear everywhere some heart thumping.

I wasn't worried about making sense in this poem because the piece of graffiti itself didn't make literal sense. I was trying more to capture the sensation of being lost that I felt when I first read it on the wall and again when I reread it in my journal. It started me thinking. If I hadn't written it down, I'd never have remembered it, nor written the poem.

There are other bonuses, too. By keeping a journal, you dedicate yourself to thinking about poems, about what they are and what yours will be, about the subjects of your poems, about their sights and sounds. You look closer at the world around you and listen with more attention. You gather the seeds of poems. You open yourself to the possible poems all around you. And there are a great many around you, just waiting to be put into words.

 PRACTICE
SESSION

1. Begin a journal. Return to the ten poems you read for the previous practice session and reread them now. Copy the best lines into your journal. Do you notice anything new in the poems? Do you respond to them differently? Do you understand them in the same way? Do they offer subjects you'll write about?

2. Over five days, write down five memories, one per day, in as much detail as you can. What makes these memories important? Who is involved? What happens? Where? When? How?

3. Take a walk through your neighborhood. Look around. Note twenty things you haven't noticed before. Include sights, sounds, smells, tastes and textures. Be specific.

4. Write down twenty uncommon words that you'd like to use in your poems. Write down their definitions, too. Save them for later use.

Sharpening the Pencil

Leo Tolstoy, the nineteenth-century Russian novelist, author of *War and Peace* and *Anna Karenina*, said, "If you ask someone: 'Can you play the violin?' and he says: 'I don't know, I have not tried, perhaps I can,' you laugh at him. Whereas about writing, people always say: 'I don't know, I have not tried,' as though one had only to try and one would become a writer."

Many want to be writers, but they never actually write their stories and poems. They never struggle with their thoughts and emotions. They never put those thoughts and emotions on paper. They never learn the craft. They never practice it. They assume that some day they'll get around to writing, and when they finally do, their stories and poems will pour out perfect the very first time. Because we use the language every day, talking with family, neighbors, friends, co-workers, because we read and write letters, because we're practiced in the language, we tend to think that all we need to do is write a poem or story and, presto, there we are, writers. But it isn't that simple or easy. If it were, there'd be no challenge. Everyone would be writing the Great American Novel or the Great American Poem. Everyone would be poet laureate for a day. That isn't the case.

Poets learn the craft and develop their skills over a period of time. For some it comes easier, for others harder, but everyone starts from scratch. Even Shakespeare served a period of apprenticeship, when he learned how to write poems and plays, how to craft the language, how to evoke its mystery and genius. While he's still, four centuries later, the preeminent writer in English, his early plays show him in the midst of his education. They're good, yes, better than plays by most other writers, but not great. His greatest works—*Hamlet, King Lear, Macbeth*, to name just three—

15

came later, after he mastered the craft. He started from scratch, learned and practiced.

Earlier I mentioned that there's much to learn. Poets are forever learning, even poets who've written and published a number of books. They read poems, study and continue to practice their craft, because each time they write, they face a new challenge: A new poem needs to be written. Each poem is a beginning. And writing poems takes practice. With each lesson learned, the poet practices to master a new technique or concept. Like dancers, musicians and painters, poets learn a new step, a new tone, a new stroke, and then practice it. There's no painting without brush strokes, no concert without tuning up, no ballet without rehearsal.

Nor are there poems without practice. Here's your first practical lesson. One of the basic forms of metaphor is "_____ of _____." The first blank is usually a concrete noun (something tangible), and the second an abstract noun (an idea or emotion; see chapter four for more on **concrete** and **abstract terms**). Start with "*a teacup of* _____." Now write a list of abstract nouns to fill in the second blank. Here's a start:

- a teacup of joy
- a teacup of sorrow
- a teacup of hope
- a teacup of despair
- a teacup of gossip
- a teacup of insult
- a teacup of silence
- a teacup of restraint
- a teacup of abandon
- a teacup of wit

Now take those abstractions in the second blank (*joy, sorrow*, etc.) and for each, list several concrete nouns to fill in the first blank. Notice that changing one part of the metaphor changes the entire metaphor. A *teacup of wit* is different from a *garden of wit* and from a *crankcase of wit*.

This is practice, but it's also play. It's fooling around, with a purpose. When you practice, you generate ideas. You experiment with the language, putting words—or sometimes just sounds—together in ways that you otherwise wouldn't. You end up writing lines and entire stanzas. You end up writing poems. You can practice metaphors, iambic pentameter and imagery. You can practice such devices of sound as **alliteration** (the repetition of initial consonant sounds, as in *brown bag*), **assonance** (the repetition of vowel sounds, as in *I rise*) and **rhyme** (the repetition of vowel and consonant sounds, as in *night light*). You can practice writing in the voice of a particular **persona** (a character you create to speak the poem, such as the coldhearted duke in Robert Browning's "My Last Duchess"). Work at these sessions. Play at them. Fool around, with the purpose of honing your skills.

Poets need to practice, because they must feel comfortable with the language, the words they use to create poems. Just as a chef practices with different spices, a carpenter practices with tools, a basketball player practices the jump shot, hook shot, layup and slam dunk, the poet practices writing to perfect the craft and to free the imagination. The more you write, the better you write. William Stafford said, "A writer is a person who enters into sustained relations with the language for experiment and experience not available in any other way." Stafford's selection of the word *sustained* is important. Writing poems is an ongoing endeavor. It's a way to think and feel, to experiment and experience, to discover what you didn't know you knew and felt. Practice, play and let these lead you to poems. Enjoy the work, so each poem, as Robert Frost said, "begins in delight and ends in wisdom."

PRACTICE SESSION

1. Create metaphors in the "_____ of _____" form. Write five versions of each of the following: *a sheen of _____, a blizzard of _____, a garden of _____, a cinder block of _____, a museum of _____*. Repeat this exercise as you like.

2. Select one of your lists of abstractions and write five new versions with new concrete nouns. Repeat this exercise as you like.

AN ASIDE:
3 ON READING POETRY

Inscribed on the door of the library at ancient Thebes was this legend: "Medicine for the soul." People came to read the plays and philosophic essays, the lyric and epic poems. They came to learn and be entertained, to be informed and to think, to experience the adventures and meditations housed there. Our situation hasn't changed much over the past two millennia. We read for those reasons, and reading continues to be a balm for our troubles and a wellspring of numerous pleasures. Medicine for the soul, indeed.

As readers, we open a book not simply to lose ourselves in it. We are caught up and carried away, but on a deeper level we become involved in experiences outside our own. We take part in other lives. We live in other eras. We explore difficulties and successes we'd never otherwise know. The written word gives us the thoughts, emotions, aspirations and deeds that have created the weave and fabric of civilization. It is our storehouse of knowledge and experience, through the ages and across cultures. It makes us human, and it makes us humane.

As poets, we read poetry to be entertained, experience the pleasures of its music, catch our breath at its drama and meditate on its reflections. We also read poetry to learn the craft. Mary Oliver, a contemporary whose poems I admire, says that "to write well it is entirely necessary to read widely and deeply. Good poems are the best teachers." All poets have favorite authors who stir their hearts, enlighten their minds, stimulate their imaginations and teach them more about the art of poetry. And this knowledge comes in addition to the pleasures poems bring.

But whose poems should you read first? We have centuries of poets and poems. We have thousands upon thousands of books. Begin with a favorite poet, with the poems that interest you most. Begin with Shakespeare's sonnets, John Keats's odes, Walt Whitman's lush poems about the heart of America, Emily Dickinson's tender, witty poems. Venture further back in time and read the ancient Sumerian epic *Gilgamesh*, the story of a king who lost his best friend to death and tried to return him to life. Read Homer's epics, *The Iliad* and *The Odyssey*. Or read *Beowulf*. Begin with what you want to read and let it lead you to other poets.

Poems have been some of my favorite teachers. I read and reread them. I read the poems of the old masters and of such strikingly different contemporary poets as Charles Wright, Rita Dove, Jorie Graham, Philip Levine, Donald Hall, Maxine Kumin, Lucille Clifton and Robert Hass. They're poets whose work I enjoy and learn from. As a reader, I delight in and admire their poems. As a poet, I study them. I read their books, and I read the literary magazines in search of their latest poems. I also seek out new poets whose poems will teach me more about the art of poetry. Whatever can be taught by a poem, I'll try to learn it.

Where should you begin? Visit the library and check out several books of poems. Visit a bookstore and browse through the selection of poetry. While you're there, browse through the current literary magazines for the newest poems by contemporary poets. Look at *Black Warrior Review*, *The Georgia Review*, *The Gettysburg Review*, *The Paris Review*, *Poetry*, *Poetry Northwest* and *Quarterly West*. There are hundreds of magazines that may interest you, and they offer a variety of poems by different poets. A good bookstore will offer a dozen or more literary magazines and several hundred books of poetry.

You may pick up a book of poems by e.e. cummings and in it see what strange, wonderful things he does with the language, as in these opening lines of an untitled poem:

> my father moved through dooms of love
> through sames of am through haves of give,
> singing each morning out of each night
> my father moved through depths of height

This is the poem's opening **stanza** (a group of lines distinct from other groups of lines; in this case a **quatrain**, a four-line stanza). Untitled poems

19

are generally known by their first lines, so this poem is commonly called "my father moved through dooms of love." It's an odd, difficult, beautiful poem, and it goes on like this for sixty-eight lines, all in honor of his father. Despite the difficulty of these lines (Do they make literal sense? Sort of, but not easily), you may notice the sounds these lines make, their music. Read them aloud, several times. Notice the assonance in the first line, the long *o* sounds in *moved*, *through* and *dooms*. Notice the **slant rhyme** (an imperfect rhyme) in the final words of the first and second lines: *love* and *give*. Notice the **true rhyme** (a perfect rhyme) in the final words in the third and fourth lines: *night* and *height*.

You may also notice that these lines, with the exception of the third, are written in a strict **meter** (a pattern of stressed and unstressed syllables; more on meter in chapter six). The meter of "my father moved through dooms of love" is iambic **tetrameter** (eight syllables of alternating unstressed and stressed syllables). Here is the meter of the first line (the capital letters indicate the stressed syllables):

my FATH- / er MOVED / through DOOMS / of LOVE

The second and fourth lines have exactly the same pattern of meter:

through SAMES / of AM / through HAVES / of GIVE,

. . . .

my FATH- / er MOVED / through DEPTHS / of HEIGHT

Despite its strange syntax, this is a formal poem, written in the long tradition of formal verse. Its strength, however, is in the music it makes, all those words put oddly together to make beautiful sounds.

When you become accustomed to the oddness of cummings's poems, you find that they do make sense, just not in an everyday fashion. He didn't want his poems to make sense in an everyday fashion; he wanted them to make sense in an innovative fashion. Cummings's poems are unconventional because he wanted the reader to experience the world in a new way, to see it with new eyes and hear it with new ears. He wanted to surprise and delight the reader. If you like e.e. cummings's poems, go back and read Emily Dickinson's poems and go on to read John Berryman's poems. If you like John Berryman's poems, read John Ashbery's poems. One poet leads you to another, and to another.

If you don't like a particular poet's work, that's OK. There's a degree of taste involved in reading poems. Some poems won't appeal to you. Set those poems aside and pick up others. Literary magazines are the best places to find a variety of poems. You may pick up an issue of *The River King Poetry Supplement*, a magazine published in Freeburg, Illinois, and in it find poems like this one by Katherine Riegel:

WHEN

in the morning a bird
rushes my window
it leaves a curious white swirl
on the glass, an outline
of its body, as though in the fright
and almost-death of the moment
part of its essence oozed out
never to be recovered.

I think of the killdeer that fakes an injury
calling loudly and limping
to lead the watcher away from its nest,
into the tall pussywillows with their feathery ears.

My lover and I call the plant "lamb's ear"
"Alex ear," because our dog's ears are that soft,
and softer. In the evening she turns
and lies down with an old man's groan, and if you get
too near her hips
she growls a warning:
I love you, but they hurt
more in the evening.
Some day they will hurt too much,
o my lovely.

If the soul
is a bird
tell it about glass,
that boundary
that looks imaginary.

The simple title "When" has an air of mystery: when what? The title invites you into the poem to discover the answers. It also serves,

21

essentially, as the first word of the poem, so it begins *When in the morning a bird. . . .* The poem is written in **free-verse** form (see chapter eight for more on **form**) and divided into four stanzas. Each of the stanzas focuses on a single subject: the first with a bird almost flying into a window, the second with another bird (or is it the same bird?) and its ruse to protect its nest, the third with the speaker's aged dog, and the fourth with the proposition that the soul is like a bird. Each of the stanzas addresses a different subject and is a complete thought, but the last stanza, in its references to "a bird" and "glass" (the window), also harkens back to the first. In a sense, the poem makes a circle. It goes from bird to killdeer to dog to soul and back to bird.

While each stanza addresses a different subject, each addresses its subject in a similar context. What the stanzas have in common, despite their different subjects, are concerns with danger, death, life and protection. The bird doesn't hit the window. The killdeer saves its young. Alex, the old dog, "growls a warning" not to cause it pain. And in the last stanza, the speaker provides a warning about dangers we cannot tell are there. The poem uses its several subjects for a singular effect. It recognizes the dangers of everyday life and urges us to be safe and compassionate, for our sake and the sake of others.

When you read poems, give your attention both to what they say and to how they say it. Notice e.e. cummings's use of sound, assonance and rhyme, and of such formal elements as meter and the quatrain stanza. Notice that Katherine Riegel writes in stanzas as well, but unlike cummings's metric four-line stanzas, her stanzas are dictated by units of thought (each stanza is a complete thought), and her lines vary from two syllables in length to fourteen. While these two poems are vastly different, you can learn from them equally. You can take what you see in them—in any poem—and apply it to your own poems. You can write a poem in iambic tetrameter with rhyme. You can write a poem that shifts from subject to subject and in the end returns to its initial subject. Whatever happens in the poems you read can happen in your poems.

In fact, when you find a poem that you especially enjoy, or a number of poems by the same poet, read them thoroughly, attentively, and sit down for a practice session: Imitate the unique style of that poet. "Before we can be poets," Mary Oliver said, "we must practice; imitation is a very good way of investigating the real thing." Don't copy poems, but don't be shy about imitating, either. Even the Welsh poet Dylan Thomas considered one of his finest poems, "Do Not Go Gentle Into

That Good Night," an imitation of William Butler Yeats's style. But that doesn't make his poem any less lovely and moving. (It's a poem you should read, along with Thomas's other fine poems.) By imitating other poets' styles, you learn more of how poems are written, and through imitation you begin to develop your own unique style.

While reading and studying poems helps you become a better writer, the main reason for reading is that poems are "Medicine for the soul." They teach and entertain. They move you and make you think. They won't give you the latest reports on international affairs or results of the local elections—no sports scores, either. But they give you just what you need, even when you don't know you need it. The American poet William Carlos Williams, one of my favorites, said it best in his poem "Asphodel, That Greeny Flower":

> It is difficult
> to get the news from poems
> yet men die miserably every day
> for lack
> of what is found there.

Let poetry work its magic on your soul. Read, enjoy, learn and write. An hour in the company of good poems is an hour in good company.

 ## PRACTICE SESSION

1. Read a book of poems or the poems in a few literary magazines. Don't rush. Spend time with the poems. This exercise may take from several days to several weeks. As you read, note in your journal which poems you like and why. Also note what you dislike. Copy your favorite lines. Note all words that interest you. Gather subjects and discover your personal concerns.

2. Read one of your favorite poems several times, at least once aloud. Imitate it however you see fit.

4 FRAMING THE HOUSE:
THE ART OF
POETRY, PART ONE

The various aspects of poetry—imagery, figures of speech, rhyme, meter, stanza form—all work at once in a poem. We discuss them singly, but none works by itself. Meter and stanza form help organize rhyme scheme. Figures of speech rely on imagery to make their comparisons vivid. Underlying each of these aspects is the language itself, the words poets use to create poems. English is a complex language, with its roots in German and graftings from the Romance languages, French, Italian and Spanish. Our words can be direct or subtle. They can be general or specific. They can appeal to the intellect and to the senses. As poets, we must understand how our words work, how they build phrases and evoke images that make poems memorable.

Building the Foundation: Plain Words and Exotic

A dozen thin strips of paper, makeshift bookmarks ripped from scratch paper, poke out from my dictionary. They mark pages where I've happened upon words that delight my ear: *brouhaha*, *glad rags*, *haberdasher*, *monkshood*, *scapegrace*, *whittlings*. I come across them by chance. While writing, I reach for my dictionary to check a spelling or look up a definition. As I run down the page in search of my listing, I find some other word that resonates. Most often it isn't a word I can use right then, but it sounds so good that I rip a strip of paper and mark the page. Later I return to it and transfer word, pronunciation and definition to my journal, adding it to the other words and notes I've collected there, for future use.

Because the word is the basic building block of the poem, you should invest in a good dictionary. I don't mean the pocket-size kinds. They're good to a point, but you give up much for the convenient size. I mean a thick dictionary, one that offers brief commentaries on the history of the English language, grammar and usage, word derivations, a dictionary that runs fifteen hundred or so pages with more words, pronunciations and definitions than you know exist. Pick up a good thesaurus, too, one thick with synonyms and antonyms. It will give you options when you search for that one just-right word. The thesaurus on my desk lists over seventeen thousand individual entries, and I've used a fair number of them.

Learn your way around the dictionary and thesaurus. Get them feeling comfortable in your hands. Consult them, even when you don't think you need to, because you'll find that they speed you on your way. The dictionary and thesaurus are reference tools, but they'll also spark ideas by offering words you didn't know you needed. They'll help you over rough spots, offer you options and teach you about the language. You'll use these tools frequently, so select good ones. The sheen has worn off the covers of both my dictionary and thesaurus. Their spines are heavily creased. Some of the pages are dog-eared and some are smudged, but this is all as it should be. They show their use, which means these tools are serving me well.

Whenever I open my dictionary, I'm ready to be surprised by a word. I have a fondness for strange and exotic words—words that make unusual sounds, words that get to the heart of things and words that have multiple meanings. There are, for instance, two listings for *cleave*, both verbs. One *cleave* means "to split or separate, as with an ax." The other means "to adhere, cling, or stick fast. Used with *to*." Among strangers at a party, I may *cleave* to Joan until I feel comfortable enough to mingle. Or I may *cleave* the crowd to reach Joan's side. Or I may write a poem that uses both words. I jot it down in my journal and write a sentence or two using *cleave*, just to practice.

The Irish poet William Butler Yeats said, "Our words must seem inevitable." He meant that every word in a poem must be the right word. The reader of a poem shouldn't have to stop in the middle of the poem and wonder why the poet used a particular word. Why that one and not this one? The poem must inspire the reader's trust. It must take the

25

reader straight through and be completely convincing the whole way. Each word must seem inevitable, the only word for that spot. This precision depends on each word being exactly the right word. Mark Twain said it in a slightly different fashion: "The difference between the *almost*-right word and the *right* word is really a large matter—it's the difference between the lightning bug and the lightning." The almost-right word gives off a little glow, but the right word lights up the sky (and the poem), illuminating everything around it. So I collect words to have the *right* word available when I need it.

While I'm fond of exotic words, they can overwhelm a poem: *azure*, *shard*, *paramour*. They're like spice in the poetic stew. Simple, everyday words are the meat and potatoes, and the poet sprinkles in the spice. Too much spice—too many exotic words—and that's all the reader notices. The spice overwhelms the poem. Make the poem as you would a hearty stew. Use everyday ingredients, everyday words, and spice it with the exotic only when the exotic adds the right flavor.

Of course, even simple, everyday words can be arranged in ways that bring out their music and magic. Here are the opening lines of Walt Whitman's "Out of the Cradle Endlessly Rocking":

> Out of the cradle endlessly rocking,
> Out of the mocking-bird's throat, that musical shuttle,
> Out of the Ninth-month midnight,
> Over the sterile sands and the fields beyond, where the child leaving
>   his bed wander'd alone, bareheaded, barefoot,
> Down from the shower'd halo,
> Up from the mystic play of shadows twining and twisting as if they
>   were alive,
> Out from the patches of briers and blackberries . . .

The first sentence of this poem—a long sentence by any standard—goes on like this for twenty-two lines about birth ("Out of the Ninth-month midnight") and the speaker's youthful days. (The poem runs two hundred and eighty-three lines in total.) At most, you'll have to look up only a couple of words in your dictionary. A few phrases are somewhat unusual: "musical shuttle," "Ninth-month midnight," "twining." They're less than common, but they aren't exotic. The poem is composed mainly of meat-and-potato words, but Whitman has arranged them to be more song than conversation. He makes the simple language sing.

Here's a complete poem by Whitman (if you haven't already, I urge you to read his poems). Again, notice the everyday language he uses:

WHEN I HEARD THE LEARN'D ASTRONOMER

When I heard the learn'd astronomer,
When the proofs, the figures, were ranged in columns before me,
When I was shown the charts and diagrams, to add, divide, and
    measure them,
When I sitting heard the astronomer where he lectured with much
    applause in the lecture-room,
How soon unaccountable I became tired and sick,
Till rising and gliding out I wander'd off by myself,
In the mystical moist night-air, and from time to time,
Look'd up in perfect silence at the stars.

These eighty-two words are fairly plain. Fifty-nine consist of a single syllable; they're common, simple words. And what a delightful poem they make.

One aspect you may notice in both poems is Whitman's use of **repetition**, a rhetorical device in which the same phrase or sentence structure is repeated, usually for emphasis. Whitman often repeats prepositional phrases ("Out of . . . " and "When . . . ") to keep his long sentences readable, and thus to keep the reader on track. He also uses repetition to build the poem: It allows him to bring new subjects in. Practice this device, repeating a grammatical structure, as a way to bring more of the world into your poems.

There's room in poems for exotic words, those that sound strangely beautiful and those that sound beautifully strange: *amorphous, expunge, ululation*. Language is the medium of poetry, as paint is the medium of painting, clay of pottery, wood of carpentry. It's the poet's responsibility to understand the medium, to understand the value of both everyday words and exotic, to know the language and how it works. The poet uses language in much the same way the carpenter uses wood: one piece at a time, one joined to another, and that joined to another, until the whole is complete and stands on its own. Just as there are exquisite details involved in carpentry, so there are exquisite details that exotic language can provide. The everyday language, however, the words we're most accustomed to, they're the mainstay of poetry.

27

They're the words that build the poem. In most poems, they're all you need, word by word, from its beginning in delight to its end in wisdom. Take delight in words, their sounds and meaning. Keep your ears open. Listen to the language. Learn how it works. Collect words and make them your own.

 ## PRACTICE SESSION

1. Collect twenty meat-and-potato words you like the sounds of. Collect ten exotic words you like the sounds of. Now write a draft using ten meat-and-potato and three exotic words. Include an avocado in the draft.

2. Write a draft about a busy intersection. Use only everyday words, slang and street language. Include a windblown newspaper in the draft.

Words Mean More Than They Say: Nuances of Meaning

When I was young, my grandparents had a poodle named Andre. He was a standard poodle, big and bounding, the type originally bred for hunting. He stood twenty-six inches at the shoulder—large, strong, fleet and brimming with energy. As a boy, I brimmed with energy, too, more so than with manners. Mischief occupied my hours. I explored the nooks and crannies of my grandparents' home: the utility room; closets packed with games, books and bric-a-brac; boxes stacked in storage; the workshop with its drills and cutting edges. Everywhere was terra incognita, unexplored land, where trouble could always be found. And my father would find me in the midst of it. Apprehended. No, Grandmother's fine stationery wasn't meant for paper airplanes. Yes, the wooden tiles of Grandfather's Scrabble game floated in the sink, but they weren't battleships. No, one did not practice with the handsaw on the legs of the workshop table.

My father's favorite expression at such times was *ornery*. He exclaimed it loudly and, when nothing was ruined, with a degree of amusement. *Ornery*, he boomed, and down the hall, tearing at full speed, a blur of ears and curls, came Andre, tail wagging, tongue lolling out, to sit proudly at my father's feet.

Because Andre mistook my father's *ornery* for *Andre* (notice the alliteration, the similar *n* and *r* sounds), I was spared a lecture on manners. Andre recognized the amusement in my father's voice and came running. *Ornery* means "having an ugly disposition; specifically stubborn and mean-spirited," but my father spoke it as a term of affection. His tone of voice reflected his use of the word. He meant *mischievous* more than he did *mean-spirited*, *playful* more than *wicked*. The distinction between what a word means and what it suggests is the difference between denotation and connotation.

Denotation is the dictionary definition of a word. It's precisely what a word means.

Connotation is the subtle shading of meanings that a word carries along with its dictionary definition. It's what a word suggests.

When we pause in conversation to search for the right word, we're really searching for just the right combination of denotation and connotation. The two go hand in hand, the literal meaning and the suggestion. Should we say, for example, that we're *pleased* with a meal or *satisfied* with it? Our choice makes a world of difference to a chef, especially to a temperamental chef. It makes a world of difference to us, too, if we're married to the chef. While the denotation may be fine, if the connotation is off, it'll be hot dogs for the rest of the week. Both *pleased* and *satisfied* denote contentment, but *satisfied* is a neutral word. It connotes a complacent fulfillment of the requirements, nothing special. *Pleased*, however, connotes delight, a sense of gratification, a glow of happiness. It's better by far to be *pleased* with a meal.

Because our language is subtler than the strict dictionary definitions of its words, poets pay attention to subtleties, to what words mean and what they suggest. What a word suggests is as important as, and often more important than, what it literally means. As they write, poets consider the numerous combinations of denotation and connotation. Then they select the word that has just the right combination of meaning and suggestion. This process often goes word by word through numerous possibilities: *satisfied, content, fulfilled, gratified, pleased*. Which should it be? Poets select each word to mean what poems need to say *and* to suggest what they need to imply.

29

To see the difference between denotation and connotation more clearly, consider these statements:

- John is firm.
- Catherine is stubborn.
- Frank is pigheaded.

All three statements denote the same thing: John, Catherine and Frank will not change their minds. We cannot sway them. But each statement connotes something quite different. *John is firm* suggests that John has good reason for not changing his mind. He listened to our arguments and exhortations, weighed them and decided to maintain his position. We can't convince him otherwise. He has the power of his convictions, and for that John deserves our admiration.

Because *Catherine is stubborn*, however, she doesn't deserve our admiration. She heard our arguments and exhortations and, despite our being right, refuses to change her mind. To be fair, Catherine may have good reason, too. But we have better reason. So we explain again, quite convincingly—to no use. Still, we may respect her resolve, even though her stubbornness leads her, mistakenly, down the wrong path.

Now the saddest of the three: *Frank is pigheaded*. He's completely wrong and, what's worse, he knows it. He's utterly unreasonable. He stands with arms crossed, a mad glint in his eyes. We'll never convince him. Our every breath is wasted. The wrong path Catherine went down mistakenly, well, Frank spins sharply on his heel and stomps down that wrong path on purpose.

The key to the subtleties of denotation and connotation can be found in those poet's tools, the dictionary and thesaurus. On my writing desk, they stand side by side, within easy reach. Should I need a word meaning *stubborn*, I flip through my thesaurus and find the heading *Stubbornness*. There I find a wealth of synonyms, words that have meanings similar to *stubborn*, and a selection of antonyms, words that have opposite meanings, such as *submission*. The thesaurus offers a multitude of ways to suggest what kind of stubbornness it is: twenty-three nouns, seven verbs and verb phrases, and fifty-five adjectives—words for every combination of denotation and connotation. *Obstinate* or *pertinacious*? *Determined* or *resolute*? *Wayward* or *headstrong*? The choice is yours, depending on which word your poem needs.

But here, a red flag of warning: Before deciding on one word or another, always reach for the dictionary to make sure you select the exact word you need. This is an absolute necessity. Check and double-check. Because each word in a poem must be the right word, never leave a selection to chance. The differences in connotations may be slight, but slight differences are the most meaningful. *Wayward* and *headstrong*, for instance, are close synonyms for *stubborn*. Both words have in common the definition *willful*. But *wayward* carries a secondary definition that distinguishes it from *headstrong*: To be *wayward* is also to be "swayed by caprice; erratic; unpredictable." This secondary definition charges *wayward* with connotations of being easily influenced, of convictions not held firmly, of opinions that change with the wind. As long as the wind blows strong and steady, *wayward* knows which way to face, but when the wind turns, *wayward* turns with it.

Poems rely as much on what they suggest as what they say. It's the power to suggest that allows poems to say much in only a few words. This makes poems concise and gives them depth. It makes poems rich with meaning. A good poem says much in those few words, and it suggests even more. That's the poem we read and read again.

PRACTICE SESSION

1. Use a thesaurus for this exercise. Select ten synonyms of the noun *pleasure*. Write a draft, ten sentences in length, using one synonym per sentence.

2. Repeat exercise one with synonyms of the noun *building*, the verb *jump*, the adjective *slow* and the verb *speed*.

3. Write a draft titled "Red" in which you give five definitions of the color, such as *Red is the heat of a summer noon*. Include one exotic word in the draft.

4. Repeat exercise three with "Blue," "Green" and "Orange."

Concrete Blocks and Fistfuls of Air: Concrete and Abstract Words

Nearly every word in the English language has a synonym meaning almost the same thing. English has an expansive, diverse vocabulary, and the differences between synonyms are often a matter of degree or style. As with *wayward* and *headstrong*, their meanings are similar but not exact. Say you wake early on a lovely Saturday morning and decide to stretch your legs. You tie your shoes, step out your door and walk. You amble, saunter, stroll, traipse, stride, strut, swagger, prance, limp, hobble, shamble, slog, stagger, reel, stumble, trek, trudge, waddle, shuffle or even tiptoe. You get where you're going, although some modes of walking are certainly more graceful than others.

The verb *walk* is a **general term**. General terms signify broad classes of persons, things and actions. The verbs listed above following *walk* are **specific terms**. They refer to individual types of walking, each more specific than the general *walk* and each different in style from the others. After *trekking* for a while through the rugged landscape of the woods, we may end up *hobbling* out. The *swagger* of the overly proud changes after a defeat to the *shuffle* of the humble.

Because English consists of such differing levels of specificity, it allows us to be more or less exact, depending on our needs. In conversation we frequently use general terms, unless we have reason to be more specific. We say we're going to a *party*. In poetry, however, the sort of party we're going to makes a great deal of difference. Is it a *ball, reception, soiree, tea, feast, gala, revel, housewarming* or *masquerade*? The poet selects the word that best serves the poem.

There are levels of general and specific terms, too: *Animal* is a general term, and *mammal* is specific compared to it, but *mammal* is general compared to *horse*, and *horse* is general compared to *roan*, and so it goes down the line until we single out the one roan mare in the east stockade. The difference between the general and the specific is often a matter of degree, from the most general to the most specific, depending on the context. Poetry favors the specific.

Another important distinction between types of words is that between **abstract terms** and **concrete terms**. Abstract terms represent ideas or qualities that are conceptual rather than tactile. We understand them intellectually. *Love*, while it affects us physically, is an abstract term, as are the words naming other emotions. They're concepts without form or body. We cannot grasp them, or see, smell, hear or taste them. Abstract terms are like fistfuls of air: We know the air is there, but we can't grasp it. For each of us, *happiness* and *sadness* mean something slightly different, and that slight difference is really quite large. What abstract terms do well is serve poems by evoking intellectual concerns quickly. A poem may speak of *pride, shame, honor, beauty, innocence, guilt* or *passion*, and the reader immediately understands the concept.

Concrete terms, on the other hand, describe qualities that are tactile: *cold*, *rough*, *salty*; *rock*, *fern*, *truck*. They appeal to the senses. They evoke images and create the landscape of the poem for the reader to see, hear, smell, taste and touch. Concrete terms provide a more immediate understanding of the poem's world by presenting it in descriptive, physical form. Good descriptive writing uses concrete terms so the reader can envision the scene: a dry creek bed, for example, mud-caked and cracked, littered with parched, brown needles fallen from the white pines that overhang it.

By their natures, concrete and specific terms go hand in hand, as do abstract and general terms. While abstract-general terms are useful in some instances, poems written primarily with abstract-general terms are diffuse and dull. They lack sensory appeal. They're as difficult to grasp as the wind. Poems written primarily with concrete-specific terms are more immediate and intimate. They draw the reader in and make a more engaging poem, one that presents details and particulars for the reader to envision. Concrete-specific terms evoke images that capture the reader's attention and imagination. Shakespeare uses concrete-specific terms in Sonnet 73 to evoke autumn, darkness, exhaustion and age:

> That time of year thou mayst in me behold
> When yellow leaves, or none, or few, do hang
> Upon those boughs which shake against the cold,
> Bare ruin'd choirs where late the sweet birds sang.
> In me thou see'st the twilight of such day
> As after sunset fadeth in the west,
> Which by and by black night doth take away,
> Death's second self, that seals up all in rest.
> In me thou see'st the glowing of such fire
> That on the ashes of his youth doth lie,
> As the death-bed whereon it must expire,
> Consum'd with that which it was nourish'd by,
> This thou perceiv'st, which makes thy love more strong,
> To love that well which thou must leave ere long.

This poem presents an eternal theme, carpe diem, Latin for *seize the day*. Through its concrete-specific terms, the poem creates images that suggest the shortness of time. The "yellow leaves" and the boughs that "shake against the cold" show the season. The birds have migrated. Winter is blowing in. It's twilight, "after sunset fadeth in the west," and the "black night doth take away" the last of the light. The fire, where "the ashes of his youth doth lie," has burned to embers (notice the metaphor "ashes of his youth") and is "Consum'd with that which it was nourish'd by." The wood that fed the fire is now the ash that extinguishes it.

In its images Sonnet 73 presents the depletion of energy and life. It goes on to state that the shortness of time makes us love more those things and people we will eventually lose. Carpe diem, seize the day, make good use of time, value what we have—that's what the poem tells us. The final urging of the poem, "To love that well which thou must leave ere long," wouldn't be as powerful without the images that precede it. We see the barren tree. We feel the cold wind that shakes its branches. We see the sun set and feel the fire lose warmth. The concrete-specific terms show us that time is short, that while we can, we must love what remains.

Most poems use both abstract-general and concrete-specific terms. It's a balancing act, but not an even one. Have your poems represent the world and its objects in concrete and specific detail. Let the reader see, hear, smell, taste and touch your poems. Appeal to the senses and the reader's attention will follow your poem wherever it leads.

PRACTICE SESSION

1. Make a list of five general terms, such as *tree, machine, clothing, reptile* and *food*. For each general word, list five specific terms (it may help to consult a thesaurus). Write a draft using one of these lists. Repeat this exercise as you like.

2. Make a list of five abstract terms, such as *liberty, good, strange, sorrow* and *pride*. For each abstract term, list five concrete examples (for *liberty*, you may have a dog off its leash, running in the park). Write a draft using one of these lists. Repeat this exercise as you like.

Touring the Grounds: Imagery

34

As I work on a draft of a poem, I pause and take it to Joan. After many years of many poems, and the numerous drafts of each, she's become an astute reader and critic. She tells me honestly what she thinks. Sometimes she tells me what I don't want to hear—that a draft isn't good. While that's disappointing to hear, it's also useful. We all need good readers and critics who point out the strengths and weaknesses of a draft. Joan is my main reader. She knows what she likes and dislikes. She's honest. I listen to her, trust her instincts and often take her suggestions. I work on the lines of the draft that she thinks weakest. One thing Joan values in poems is their appeal to her senses. She likes poems she can see and hear and feel. She likes the sights, sounds and textures of a poem. She dislikes unwieldy abstractions, poems full of abstract-general terms. They don't give rise to emotions. They're too large and amorphous. Images, on the other hand, give rise to emotions by presenting real things-in-words that she responds to.

What Joan responds to is the **imagery**, not the statement. Statements tell about things, but they're flat and not very interesting. *He loves her* tells us something, but not much. If he kneels before her and takes her hand in his, that shows us more. It presents tactile information. It shows us a tender moment, an act of submission, a caress. It's an image we respond to because we witness it.

Images allow the reader to witness the world of the poem clearly and sharply. They show the world in specific, particular detail. An image begins with a thing, a concrete term—a field, for example. *Field*, however, is a general term. This may be any sort of field. But with further description, it becomes more specific. With furrows, it becomes a cultivated field, part of a farm. Now add corn and describe what stage of growth the corn is in. Is it knee-high? Has it tasseled? Is it all broken stalks? The condition of the corn shows us the season without us having to be told. If the field is stubbled with broken stalks, it's after the harvest, autumn. With a dusting of snow between the furrows, it becomes early winter. The power of images rise from particular, relevant details.

We tend to think of images as visual, but in poetic terms, an image is a word or a phrase that presents *any* sensory details for the reader to experience. They may be visual (sight), auditory (sound), tactile (touch), olfactory (smell), gustatory (taste) or any combination of these. Most images affect more than one of our senses. As you read poems, take in the images, the sensory details. Linger over them. Imagine them, and in your imagining, feel them. Here's a poem by Margot Schilpp, a contemporary poet. Read it slowly. Let your imagination fully experience its images. Let your senses delight in your imagination.

35

ONE SUNDAY EACH SPRING

So quickly we're transported, the field a yellow cathedral:
    the strict rows of daffodils riffle up a pollen breeze,
        the barn yawns another annotation,

and the farmhouse, distant, tiny, props itself
    against the sky. Never mind that now the gentle mounds
        are left untilled, or that the farm, idle

for years, produces nothing but the remembrance
    of itself. Each April those old bulbs fracture
        again, all the pedicels again support glorious blooms,

and I am dressed up: pink gingham, patent leather,
    an empty Easter basket slung over my six-year-old arm.
        All the trees pass in furious motion—green touches glass,

the road narrows to dirt, then dead-end, and our family
    erupts from the car—we spend an hour
        working up the rows. See my nose, dusted yellow,

disappointed again each year when there's no aromatic reward
    from those flowers cultivated for size and number.
        Hear my hands slide down the hollow stalks,

my squeal at the eerie squeak of the stems as I pull.
    Feel the crust of mud caking my mary-janes, the soles now
        moon-boot sized and heavy stepping. Rains

must have moved across the state's southern tip
    last night, left the land too wet; we struggle
        to stitch ourselves into the rows, our arms still

flexing mechanically, a rhythmic clutch and transfer.
    And we find it is enough. The car fills with a brown
        odor of earth top-noted by green and yellow,

with wet newspaper, with the stems' weepy milk, and all
    of what rises again from the farm, the disappearing
        road, the last uneasy visit to the empty tomb of that field.

Notice the concrete-specific terms the poem uses: *yellow*, *daffodils*, *breeze*, *barn*, one quickly after another. The poem is rich with images, and they appeal to all five senses. The images create the scene so well that the reader can smell the soil, feel the wind, hear the squeak of wet flower stems and taste the pollen. The images create the world of the poem so well that the reader walks the rows with the speaker on this spring Sunday.

Images are not simply decoration. They aren't simply descriptions of things. What a poem shows, and how the poem shows it, imparts meaning, both emotional and intellectual. It creates overtones. It suggests. The first line of "One Sunday Each Spring" does just that in the phrase "the field a yellow cathedral," which is also a metaphor (as you'll see in chapter six, similes and metaphors rely on well-crafted images). It is Sunday, after all, and this visit to the old farm with its "yellow cathedral" is a sort of worship, a pilgrimage. It's a holy experience, a reverent farewell.

The imagery of "One Sunday Each Spring" is lush and highly descriptive, but some poems work better with starker, leaner images. This poem by Tim Geiger, another contemporary poet, has a completely different feel:

BUILDING A NEW HOME

The generator kicks and whines,
steam shovel treads grind limestone
to dust; hydraulics, hammers,
and someone on the roof shouting
orders for more shingles.

          I got up at dawn,
the first blue light anointing
the loose clouds, the sweating back,
both eyes burning, essential salt
leaking down my scalp.

          New buildings
break away from the red broken clay.
Excavation before foundation—
five thousand nails per plywood frame.
We're working towards something
better—full of daylight, and easy
to enter.

> This must be
> the song my father taught me:
> build each one as if it were my own,
> take care of my tools—hammer,
> drill, the silver saw-blade edge—
> they are the only things that matter
> in this world, they will make me
> known among these men.

The imagery here is more concise, more directly functional, but it's just as concrete and specific, just as evocative. These images fit the poem and its subject. The first image ("The generator kicks and whines") sets the scene and creates action. The images that follow do likewise. They're images of action rather than description. Like the labor they present, they waste no motion. They're smooth and efficient, to the point, which is to show the work of building a house. The images complement the subject. They also suggest more than they say. The phrase "five thousand nails per plywood frame" is an especially effective image: We see the hammer swing and hear the crack as it strikes nail, all without the poem ever directly saying so.

The subjects of Geiger's and Schilpp's poems are vastly different, and their images reflect that. Geiger's images are active and sparse, while Schilpp's are detailed and lush—each to its purpose. Images must serve the poem. If they aren't relevant, if they're only decoration, then they clutter up the poem. They're laundry scattered across the room or, worse, litter on the roadside. But well-crafted images are valuable. They present the world of the poem and invite the reader into it. They give the reader points of reference. They present specific details the reader responds to. Images serve the poem best by making its world concrete and specific and by directing the reader's attention to what's important.

PRACTICE SESSION

1. Stop somewhere you don't usually stop. For ten minutes, note the sensory details of that place. Make use of all five senses and be precise.

2. Write a draft describing a color photograph. Begin with a wide-angle view, then focus on a specific person or object in the photograph. End the draft by describing the color in the background.

3. Write a draft about a room you haven't been in for at least ten years. Make use of all five senses.

4. Write a draft, at least thirty lines in length, about traveling to a place you've never been. Consult a map if it helps. Why are you going there? Do you travel by car, plane, train, bobsled? What sights do you see on the way? What sounds, smells, textures and tastes? Who will meet you there?

5

AN ASIDE:
ON THE
FUSSY DETAILS

Betty Becker stood a smidge over five feet. She was slight of build and slow of step. She wore a shawl. Her gray hair was wrapped tight in a bun. Her voice quavered, the mild hesitations that come with age. And I cowered before her. Six weeks into my high school Senior English class, she padded down the aisles and returned our midterm essays, with comments of praise and dispraise. At the back of the room, she stopped to pay special attention to me. "If I were your mother," she said loudly, and my classmates watched as I withered under her attention, "I'd have you over my knee for such poor performance." Despite the quaver in her voice, she had lost none of her authority. She held out my essay, with a grade I'd rather forget marked large in red ink. "English," she sniffed, "is your native tongue, is it not?" The pages of my essay looked like a road map, red highways shooting across its pages linking major metropolitan centers of errors. My grammar and punctuation were terrible, and Betty Becker vowed before the class that I was her pet project for the rest of the semester.

As an editor, I read poems submitted to *The Gettysburg Review* with the exacting standards that Betty Becker succeeded, finally, in teaching me. Some poems submitted to the review show imagination, but they're poorly written. Their sloppy grammar and punctuation betray them. (I imagine Betty Becker shuddering in the presence of such poor performance in these poems.) Imagination is the lifeblood of poetry, but poems must be well written for the imagination to shimmer and shine. Language is the medium of the art, and faulty grammar and punctuation make for faulty art. Mary Oliver notes, "A poem that is composed without the sweet and correct formalities of language, which are what sets it apart from the dailiness of ordinary writing, is doomed. It will not fly."

Little in the world of arts and letters is as dreadful as a poorly written poem. Either the reader labors doggedly to get through it—bless the soul of such a reader—or sets it quickly aside. Neither is the response we seek. The poem has failed, and whatever sterling imagination has shaped it is negated.

The mechanics of writing—the conventions of grammar and punctuation—are important. Some beginning writers think of grammar and punctuation as restrictive, binding, as though they're straitjackets, as though they hamper the imagination. Such writers value the content of poetry over its craft. But that's like valuing the physique of a dancer over the grace of the dance. Good poetry doesn't choose between imagination and craft. It chooses both. The imagination is expressed in language, and proper grammar and punctuation provide clarity to the language. They make sense of the words that create the poem. They help the reader enjoy, instead of stopping to puzzle out what the words are supposed to mean. They provide the fluid grace that makes poetry memorable.

Some poems do break the conventions. They make use of odd syntax and irregular punctuation. Some have no punctuation at all. Read any of e.e. cummings's poems—for example, "next to of course god america i"—and you'll see broken conventions aplenty. But he doesn't break conventions willy-nilly; he does so to create certain effects, a pause, or a poem spoken at breakneck speed. Other poets do the same, for effect, when a poem calls for it. That's key: Do what the poem calls for. Most poems call for standard grammar and punctuation. Breaking the conventions does the poem good only when there's reason to break the conventions, which means you must first know the conventions to understand when it's beneficial to break them.

Because you use them daily in conversation, you already know most of the conventions. When you're in doubt, logic and intuition usually point the proper way. The written word, however, is more exact than the spoken word. Errors appear more glaring on the page. In conversation, context makes clear the difference between *its* and *it's*. The former is the possessive form of the pronoun *it*; the latter is the contraction of *it is*. *Its* and *it's* are **homophones**, words with the same sound but different spellings and meanings. In conversation, we tell them apart easily enough, but on the page, the wrong word sticks out like a circus clown at a church service. It draws the reader's attention and disapproval: *Its nine o'clock. The elm shed it's leaves.* If the language is flawed, the poem is flawed. It doesn't say what it's supposed to say. And where there's one mistake, there are bound to be others. How can the reader trust the poem now? Trust is essential. The reader must never doubt the poem.

Recall what Mary Oliver said: "A poem that is composed without the sweet and correct formalities of language . . . is doomed. It will not fly." Ezra Pound, the great expatriate poet, said, "Poetry must be as well written as prose." If you won't abide sloppy, incorrect prose, don't abide sloppy, incorrect poetry. Poetic license doesn't justify careless writing. Certainly, you may break the conventions of grammar and punctuation to achieve certain effects, if they make the poem better, but you must know the conventions to understand why breaking them makes the poem better. If you break the conventions wisely, the reader senses the motivation and intelligence of that decision. If you break the conventions unwisely, all the reader sees is a mistake.

If you can use a refresher course, or even if you feel confident in your writing, check your library or bookstore for a good primer. You'll find many good ones, and any will suffice. I recommend two books by Karen Elizabeth Gordon: *The Well-Tempered Sentence* (on punctuation) and *The Transitive Vampire* (on grammar). They are the most educational and entertaining primers on grammar and punctuation I've come across. These funny and wise books will teach you well and make you laugh. (They have been expanded and revised and are now titled *The New Well-Tempered Sentence* and *The Deluxe Transitive Vampire*. Whichever editions you choose, they'll benefit your writing.) I've read and reread these invaluable resources, and I continue to consult them when I have doubts about proper usage.

Sometimes, in trying to achieve meter or in the blink of a line break, the poet loses track of a sentence. Always look to the sentence first, then take care of the formal aspects of the poem. For a quick study, here are common errors in poems I've recently read. This isn't by any means a comprehensive list, nor are the items listed in any particular order. By learning to avoid these errors, you'll be on your

42

way to mastering the conventions of the English language, and that's part of writing good poems.

Wrong word. Mistaking one word for another is all too common, either because the words are homophones (such as *there, they're* and *their*) or because an important nuance distinguishes one from another. *Lie* and *lay* are examples of the latter: *Lie* means to rest in a horizontal position, while *lay* means to set down. After I lay a book on my bedside table, I lie down for a nap. When in doubt about the proper word, check your dictionary.

Plural and possessive. The plural of a word is formed by adding an *s* (or *es* in some instances) to the word; the possessive is formed by adding an *'s*, and the plural possessive is formed by adding an *s'*. If you are to dine with Mr. and Mrs. Smith in their home, you are dining at the Smiths' (plural possessive), not at the Smith's (singular possessive). An exception is the possessive of *it*, which is *its*, not the contraction *it's*.

Misplaced modifiers. A modifier is a word or phrase that defines or describes a noun (or, in the case of an adverb, a verb). It must be placed properly to modify the right noun. If you have *a man sweeping the floor with a long white beard*, pity him his lack of a broom. Or place the modifier where it belongs: *a man with a long white beard, sweeping the floor.*

Dangling modifiers. When the noun a modifier should modify is absent, you have a dangling modifier: *Waking at dawn, the sunrise was beautiful.* The trouble here is that the sunrise does not wake; the modifier *waking at dawn* applies to the person who sees beauty in the sunrise. The sentence can be rewritten *Waking at dawn, she saw a beautiful sunrise.*

Subject-verb agreement. The subject and verb must agree. *I write; you write; he writes; we write; they write.* Beware of words that come between the subject and verb: A *flock* of sparrows *feeds* on the bread crumbs Joan scatters in our backyard. The subject is *flock*, not *sparrows*.

Pronoun agreement. A pronoun must agree in number with the noun it represents. The common error is the use of a plural pronoun where a singular pronoun is needed. In the sentence *Everyone should say what they think*, the plural pronoun *they* disagrees with the singular *everyone*. The sentence should read *Everyone should say what he thinks*, or

43

Everyone should say what she thinks (also notice that the verb *think* becomes *thinks* to agree with the pronoun).

Comma splice. When a comma joins two sentences without a conjunction (*and*, *but*, *or*, etc.), you have a comma splice: *They went downtown to see a movie, it started at eight.* The comma after *movie* should be a period, and *it* begins a new sentence. When the sentences are short and closely related, however, a comma splice is acceptable: *He said no, she said yes.*

Run-on sentence. A run-on sentence is similar to a comma splice except no comma appears between the sentences: *They went downtown to see a movie it started at eight.* The sentences are run together. The correction is the same: a period after *movie*, and *it* begins a new sentence.

These are common errors, and each is easily corrected. All it takes is an understanding of the conventions of grammar and punctuation to achieve "the sweet and correct formalities of language." Proper grammar and punctuation keep your poems clean and readable. They keep the reader on track. They don't hinder the imagination; on the contrary, they allow it to shine in all its grace and glory.

6 FURNISHING THE HOUSE:
THE ART OF POETRY, PART TWO

A poem must have emotional and intellectual qualities that compel the reader from first line to last. But a poem needn't be on an epic subject. It needn't make grand, sweeping statements. It needn't—and generally shouldn't—be melodramatic, fraught with high emotion. The more true to life the poem's subject, the better the poem. It can be about putting a child to bed, mowing the lawn or shopping for groceries—common, everyday subjects. More important is *how* the poem expresses its subject. The English poet A.E. Housman said, "Poetry is not the thing said but a way of saying it." There lies the art of poetry: in the manner, style and grace of its expression. Imagery is part of the *how*, as are figures of speech, the devices of sound, rhyme and meter. They contribute to the grace of poetic expression. They are the furnishings that make the poetic house a place to live.

Furniture That Fits: Figures of Speech

One way a poem expresses its subject is through **figures of speech**, phrases that evoke images *and* lay a figurative level of meaning onto the literal level. Sometimes ornate, sometimes startlingly simple, they accent a poem, as well as express it. They create a sense of vigor and originality. They reveal the imagination at work and at play. They create emphasis, present memorable images and describe through association. And because figures of speech work through implication, they allow poems to say much in only a few words. Remember, economy and resonance are the hallmarks of poetry: a few words that say much.

Good poems involve the reader. While an artfully rendered direct statement can swell with passion ("Christ, that my love were in my arms, / And I in my bed again!"), direct statements are usually informative and dull. They treat the reader as a passive bystander. Figures of speech draw the reader into the poem. By their nature, they make images that appeal to the senses and invite the reader to make associations. They imply, the reader infers, and thus the reader becomes a participant in the poem.

The most common figures of speech are **simile** and **metaphor**. A simile shows similarity between two things that are otherwise not similar. (The term *simile* comes from the Latin *similis*, which means "of the same kind.") Similes work by explicitly comparing one thing to another through the words *like* or *as*. The Scottish poet Robert Burns, for example, begins his poem "A Red, Red Rose" with two similes:

> O my Luve's like a red, red rose,
>   That's newly sprung in June:
> O my Luve's like the melodie
>   That's sweetly play'd in tune.

Immediately, the reader has two comparisons to think about and enjoy: The speaker's love is like a rose and like a melody. Notice that similes employ images. The rose involves visual, olfactory and tactile images: A rose looks beautiful, smells fragrant, and its petals feel velvety. The melody involves an auditory image, music, and a tactile image, if you consider that melody may lead to dancing cheek to cheek. These similes are more descriptive and enjoyable than the speaker simply saying his love is pretty, smells good, has soft skin and a sweet voice. That's all nice, but it isn't interesting and doesn't make for good poetry. It's the most abstract and bland sort of description. Similes, on the other hand, allow poets both to show and imply what they mean. The reader sees the comparison, thinks about it and understands it. The reader takes an active role in comprehending the poem, which is more enjoyable for the reader.

While a simile explicitly compares one thing to another, a metaphor implicitly compares, without use of the words *like* or *as*. (The term *metaphor* comes from the Greek *metapherein*, which means "to transfer.")

46

A metaphor transfers the attributes of one thing to another. In essence, it equates one thing with another. Instead of presenting similarity, as "my Luve's like a red, red rose" does, a metaphor equates: "my Luve is a red, red rose." The speaker's love isn't *like* a rose; she *becomes* a rose, with all the rose's pleasant associations and attributes. The Greek philosopher Aristotle said that "the greatest thing by far is to be a master of metaphor . . . it is also a sign of genius, since good metaphor implies an intuitive perception of the similarity in dissimilars." Samuel Johnson noted that metaphor "is a great excellence in style . . . for it gives you two ideas for one."

Metaphors are created in a number of ways. One noun can be associated with another noun through the preposition *of* (as shown in chapter four): a teacup of joy, a teacup of sorrow. A noun can be associated with another noun through the verb *to be*: "History is a clumsy cape," writes Kathleen Halme in her poem "Every Substance Is Clothed." In this metaphor, the abstraction *history* becomes something concrete, a cape. It trails behind us. We wear it, taking it with us wherever we go. Because history in this case is a "clumsy" cape, it gets in our way. It encumbers and limits us, as the past can limit the present.

Metaphors can be created through verbs that have specific applications: "Dreamy cars graze on the dewy boulevard," writes James Tate in his poem of that title. The verb *graze* describes how cattle feed. Here it implies that the cars are cattle meandering along the boulevard. They're big, bulky, and move slowly, aimlessly. Notice that the adjective *dewy* reinforces the metaphor's image: The boulevard is a dewy field early in the morning.

A single metaphoric concept may even run throughout a poem in a sequence of related metaphors. In such a case, called an **extended metaphor**, the sequence is highly developed, and numerous associations are brought forth. Robert Frost called metaphor "saying one thing in terms of another." Extended metaphor makes an entire soliloquy of that saying. Reread Shakespeare's Sonnet 18 ("Shall I compare thee to a summer's day?"), which appears on pages 9–10, and note its sequence of metaphors. It makes use of an extended metaphor that relates the poem's subject to various aspects of summer. The metaphor extends throughout the poem.

While simile and metaphor are the most common figures of speech, others will also benefit your poems. **Overstatement** (also called *hyperbole*) is exaggeration used for emphasis or humor. When the speaker of

47

Christopher Marlowe's "The Passionate Shepherd to His Love" says, "And I will make thee beds of roses / And a thousand fragrant posies," he uses overstatement in trying to convince a woman of his love. Their life together, his overstatement wishfully implies, will be a bed of roses.

The opposite of overstatement is **understatement**, which presents something as less than it actually is. Understatement creates emphasis because the reader perceives the difference between what is said and what is. When the speaker of Dorothy Barresi's "The Jaws of Life" says, "You think life owes you—what? Happiness? / A certain modicum of headache relief?" the reader sees the difference between a desire for happiness and a desire for "headache relief." Sometimes all we would like is to be free of the pounding between our temples. Perhaps life doesn't owe us happiness; freedom from pain will suffice. That difference is effective understatement.

Paradox is a statement that at first seems contradictory but is nonetheless true, as in these lines from Shakespeare's Sonnet 138: "When my love swears that she is made of truth, / I do believe her, though I know she lies." While the speaker knows she lies, he chooses to believe her. Love does that; we ignore what, perhaps, we shouldn't. Her lies are more beautiful than the truth.

Metonymy substitutes one thing for another. Christina Rossetti's "A Life's Parallels" begins, "Never on this side of the grave again." Here, as in other poems, *the grave* is a substitute for *death*. The term used as a substitute must be closely associated with the term it stands for to make the association readily apparent. Because the grave is closely associated with death, it stands in well.

Synecdoche is a special type of metonymy. It uses a part to represent the whole, as in Samuel Taylor Coleridge's "The Pains of Sleep": "Ere on my bed my limbs I lay." The term *limbs* represents the entire body. Synecdoche may also use the whole to represent a part. In Shakespeare's play *Antony and Cleopatra*, the term *Egypt* often refers to Cleopatra, the queen of Egypt. The whole represents a part.

Synaesthesia describes something usually perceived by one sense in terms of another sense. In "The Garden," Andrew Marvell writes, "a green thought in a green shade," describing things felt—*thought* and *shade*—in terms of vision. In "I Heard a Fly Buzz," Emily Dickinson writes, "With Blue—uncertain stumbling Buzz," describing something seen, *Blue*, in terms of sound.

You'll find uses for all these figures of speech, but you'll likely write similes and metaphors most often. Beware, however, the **mixed metaphor,** a metaphor in which the elements are incongruous, as in "His proposition ran aground on the brick wall of her refusal." The mistake here is that a metaphoric ship (his proposal) may run aground on a reef, a shoal or a shore, but not on a brick wall. All three words—*reef, shoal* and *shore*—fix the metaphor nicely. Each also provides alliteration with the main word of the metaphor, *refusal*: The *r* of *reef* and *shore* and the *l* of *shoal* create an echo with the *r* and *l*, respectively, of *refusal*. The alliteration unifies the metaphor through its echoes.

The art of simile and metaphor doesn't lie in extravagant complications, not even in extended metaphors, but in clean, clear, crisp associations. "All the world's a stage," writes Shakespeare in his play *As You Like It.* In "The Unbeliever," Elizabeth Bishop writes, "asleep he curled / in a gilded ball." In "For the Union Dead," Robert Lowell writes of "a Sahara of snow." These are insightful figures of speech. They present strong images, make interesting sounds and, in their associations, create levels of meaning. For every figure of speech you use in a poem, you may write five, ten or twenty versions of it, but the work— the play—is well worth it. Good figures of speech enrich your poems beyond measure.

 **PRACTICE SESSION**

1. Write five versions, as quickly as you can, of each of the following. Don't worry about making sense. When you finish, put a check by the similes that interest you most.

> The snow fell like _____ .
> Like a _____ , he whisked the broom across the floor.
> Lovely as a _____ , she danced a fluid waltz.
> He was as puzzled as _____ .
> In her dream a sparrow, like a _____ , alit on a porch rail.

2. Write a paragraph describing in detail one of your favorite possessions. Write another paragraph describing in detail a good friend. Now

write a draft about the friend in terms of the object. Write a draft about the object in terms of the friend.

3. Write a draft about your first romance. Use, in this order, over-statement, paradox, synecdoche, understatement and synaesthesia. Include the title and a lyric from a popular song of that time.

Rooms With Echoes: Devices of Sound

Sometimes, listening to someone speak, I lose myself in the voice. Whether strong and assertive or mellow and melodic doesn't matter; the voice itself carries me along like a leaf on a stream. Sometimes I don't even hear the words. The sounds enchant me. Poetry works that way. Sounds are another part of *how* a poem says what it says. The sounds a poem makes are its music, the lilt and echo that charm the reader. Originally, poetry was an oral art. Poems were recited to audiences gathered specifically to hear poems. (These events still take place. Look for poetry readings in your area.) Now poetry reaches a wider audience through print. Still, when you read poems, read them aloud and listen to their music. At the very least, sound them out in your mind as you read. Develop an inner ear that hears what your eyes see. Listen closely. Music makes the poem and, as the English poet Samuel Taylor Coleridge wrote, one sign of genius in a poet is a "delight in richness and sweetness of sound."

You need not understand the elements of sound—fricatives (*f* and *v* sounds), plosives (*b* and *p* sounds) and such. Linguists take care of those. But you must be aware of the language and listen to its sounds and echoes. Read these lines from Alexander Pope's long poem *An Essay on Criticism* and hear the sounds they make:

> True ease in writing comes from art, not chance,
> As those move easiest who have learned to dance.
> 'Tis not enough no harshness gives offence,
> The sound must seem an Echo to the sense:
> Soft is the strain when Zephyr gently blows,
> And the smooth stream in smoother numbers flows;
> But when loud surges lash the sounding shore,
> The hoarse, rough verse should like the torrent roar:
> When Ajax strives some rock's vast weight to throw,
> The line too labours, and the words move slow;

Not so, when swift Camilla scours the plain,
Flies o'er th' unbending corn, and skims along the main.

The eye moves quicker than the lips, but it recognizes rather than intones. If you read these lines silently, read them aloud now and linger over the sounds. Hear the music they make.

This passage is itself a lesson in the art of writing poetry. Its subject is the use of sound to complement sense: "The sound must seem an Echo to the sense." Notice how easily "And the smooth stream in smoother numbers flows" slips from the lips. Notice how patiently you must articulate "But when loud surges lash the sounding shore, / The hoarse, rough verse should like the torrent roar." Because the sounds clash, they require precise utterance, and that precision gives those lines a loud energy. Notice how slowly you must enunciate "When Ajax strives some rock's vast weight to throw, / The line too labours, and the words move slow." The sounds reproduce the deliberate effort it takes to heave a great stone.

This passage also illustrates two styles of sound: **euphony** and **cacophony**. Euphony is a combination of sounds that please the ear, such as "Soft is the strain when Zephyr gently blows." The sounds flow smoothly by. Cacophony is a combination of sounds that grate on the ear, such as "When Ajax strives some rock's vast weight to throw." The *j*, *x* and *k* sounds are harsh and jarring. Poems generally make use of euphony. They strive for grace and beauty, using euphony to achieve those aims. But cacophony also plays a role. When the sense calls for it, cacophony achieves dramatic results. The American poet Randall Jarrell uses it effectively in "The Death of the Ball Turret Gunner" when the gunner, sleeping at his guns as his B-29 flies over enemy territory, wakes to "black flak and the nightmare fighters." The discordant double *k* sound of "black flak" staggers him—blam, blam—and staggers the reader, too.

The music of poetry comes from putting sounds together in certain combinations, either for euphony or cacophony, whichever the poem needs at a particular spot. The main devices of sound are alliteration, assonance, consonance and onomatopoeia.

Alliteration is the repetition of identical consonant sounds: "And the smooth stream in smoother numbers flows." It may occur anywhere within the words—the beginning, middle or end—and it may occur in one line or over a number of lines. But take care with alliteration. It

51

occurs naturally, without your purposefully using it. In fact, you'd have to work to avoid it. When used to excess, alliteration ends up like a bad newspaper headline: "Mad Monkey Makes Mulch of Metropolis." Too much alliteration sounds clunky and overwrought. It draws attention to itself and away from the poem. Ironically, alliteration works best when the reader doesn't consciously notice it. Save it for special occasions, when it serves the poem by tying together important words, like "black flak." Used rarely, and well, alliteration creates emphasis and unexpected music.

Assonance is the repetition of identical vowel sounds: "Soft is the strain when Zephyr gently blows." Like alliteration, assonance occurs naturally and can be used to excess. But vowel sounds are softer than consonant sounds and tend to glide by. The key to assonance is noticing the predominant vowel sounds and modulating them. Notice in the line quoted above that both preceding and following the *e* sounds are *o* sounds, in "Soft" and "blows." Neither vowel sound overpowers the line. The *o* gives way to the *e*, and the *e* gives way back to the *o*. Because English vowels can be pronounced a number of ways, the spelling of a word doesn't always guide you in creating assonance. The vowel *a*, for example, is pronounced differently in *pat*, *pay*, *care* and *far*. Don't trust the spelling of a word; trust your ear.

Consonance is alliteration taken one step farther: Two or more consonant sounds are repeated in words with dissimilar vowel sounds. In "The sound must seem an Echo to the sense," consonance occurs in the *s* and *n* sounds of *sound* and *sense*. The consonants make similar sounds; the vowels make different sounds. Such combinations as *chatter* and *chitter*, *dope* and *dupe*, and *flick* and *flock* employ consonance.

Onomatopoeia is the use of words that imitate sounds and suggest their meaning, as does *lash* in "But when loud surges lash the sounding shore." English is rich with words that can be used for onomatopoeia: *Buzz*, *crack*, *hiss*, *murmur*, *sizzle*, *snap* and *whirr* are only a few. Onomatopoeia is effective because the words reproduce natural sounds. They sound out what they mean.

The effects of sound always work with context. Alliteration and assonance can tie important words—and their ideas—together. The metaphor "the shoal of her refusal," for example, makes use of alliteration to unify its parts through sound: shoa*l* and refusa*l*. Meaningful sound takes two words and unites them in a single compact idea. As you write, listen to your words. The best way to develop a good ear is to write and hear, over and over. When you write an important word, listen to its sounds, then write words that repeat those sounds. Working together in a poem, your meaningful sounds will create music.

PRACTICE SESSION

1. Write a draft with the word *round* in the first line. In at least every other line, repeat the *o* sound of *round* twice. Repeat this exercise with the words *stay*, *feed*, *pie* and *boot*. In each draft include an image of an urban landscape.

2. Write a draft with the word *bother* in the first line. In alternate lines, repeat the *b* and *th* sounds, respectively, twice per line. Repeat this exercise with the words *cane*, *steal*, *fog* and *ward*. In each draft include a metaphor and one exotic word.

Rings and Chimes: Rhyme

The best known device of sound is **rhyme**, the repetition of vowel and consonant sounds. It's what our grade-school teachers taught us poetry is: lines that rhyme. But rhyme isn't all there is to poetry. Over the course of years, rhyme comes in and goes out of fashion. For much of the twentieth century, rhyme has been out of fashion, used only in special situations, as other devices of sound are, to tie important words together through sound.

Recent years, however, have seen rhyme coming back into fashion. While contemporary poets don't feel obligated to rhyme their poems, at least not consistently, a growing number make use of rhyme. It's a guide that helps them through the numerous drafts of their poems. It helps them organize and discover. Then, in the finished poems, rhyme is a guide that leads the reader through. Whichever sort of poet you are, an always rhymer or occasional rhymer, it's helpful to understand the various types of rhyme.

The twelve-line passage from Pope's *An Essay on Criticism* (on pages 50-51) makes use of six rhymes: *chance-dance*, *offence-sense*, *blows-flows* and so on. These are **true rhymes**, repeating identical vowel and consonant sounds in identical patterns. True rhyme occurs in the stressed syllables of words: ofFENSE and SENSE. For true rhyme to occur in words of multiple syllables, the unstressed syllables following the stressed syllables must also rhyme, as in GLORious and vicTORious. True rhyme rings true. The reader hears it immediately.

Slant rhyme differs from true rhyme in that its sounds are similar rather than identical. Slant rhyme, also called *near rhyme* and *off rhyme*, substitutes alliteration or assonance in place of true rhyme. The pairing of *dove* and *groove* is a slant rhyme that substitutes alliteration: The consonant sound *v* is repeated exactly, but the vowel sounds preceding it are similar, not exact. The pairing of *mate* and *sake* is a slant rhyme that substitutes assonance: The vowel sound *a* is repeated exactly, but the consonant sounds following it are similar, not exact. Slant rhyme misses true rhyme by just a hair, but sounds close enough that the reader hears the echo.

Consonance, discussed on page 52, is a particular kind of slant rhyme. Multiple consonant sounds are repeated with different vowel sounds, as in *speak* and *spook*, *tell* and *till*, and *roam* and *room*.

One other kind of slant rhyme, called **apocopated rhyme**, uses true rhyme sounds, but both rhymes don't fall on stressed syllables. Instead, apocopated rhyme falls on a stressed syllable in one word and an unstressed syllable in the other, as in *bow* and *fallow* (BOW, FALlow).

The location of rhyming syllables is important, too. **Masculine rhyme** occurs in single-syllable words, as in *chance* and *dance*, and in the stressed final syllables of polysyllabic words, as in *account* and *surmount* (acCOUNT, surMOUNT). **Feminine rhyme** occurs in words of two or more syllables in which the rhyming last syllables are unstressed, as in *hackle* and *rental* (HACKle, RENTal). Masculine and feminine rhymes create different effects. Masculine rhyme, because it ends on stressed syllables, creates a forceful sound, like the crack-snap of a branch broken across the knee. Feminine rhyme falls gently away, like a stately bow and curtsy after a waltz. Each has its use, depending on the poem's subject and the context of the rhyme.

For the best effect, rhyming words must appear with regularity, as they do in a **rhyme scheme** (a pattern of rhyme; more on rhyme schemes in chapter eight), or they must appear near each other, because too great a separation between rhymes loses the effect. Just as the location of rhyming syllables is important to the sound of a rhyme, the location of the rhyming words themselves is important. **End rhyme** appears at the end of two or more lines, as in the passage from Pope's *An Essay on*

Criticism. **Internal rhyme** appears in the middle of one or more lines. It may be matched with an end rhyme, as Coleridge does in "The Rime of the Ancient Mariner": "The ice did *split* with a thunder-*fit*." It may match two words in the middle of a line, as Christina Rossetti does in "Sleeping at Last": "Cold and *white*, out of *sight* of friend and of lover." It may match words in the middle of two lines, as Matthew Arnold does in "Philomela": "Dost thou *tonight* behold, / Here, through the *moon-light* on this English grass, / The unfriendly palace in the Thracian wild?" (Also notice the internal slant rhyme of "grass" and "palace.") Internal rhyme is less noticeable than end rhyme, but it serves a similar purpose. It rings and chimes, uniting words and ideas, and helps create a unified aural experience for the reader.

Now a few words of warning: Too often rhyme appears in a simplistic *moon-June* fashion. We've all heard such lifeless rhymes. They make rhyme seem obligatory instead of inspired. When rhyme is treated as an ornament of poetry, a bauble, it doesn't serve the poem. When the reader can predict a rhyme, as in *moon* and *June*, the rhyme fails completely. Rhyme should be unexpected. Like the poem itself, rhyme should surprise and delight the reader.

You can practice rhyme, and the other devices of sound, by putting words together and listening to the sounds they make, the way the sound of one word is echoed in a subsequent word. The late poet and teacher Richard Hugo wrote that "as a young poet I set an arbitrary rule that when I made a sound I felt was strong, a sound I liked specially, I'd make a similar sound three to eight syllables later. Of course it would often be a slant rhyme." In many ways, as you write, you'll find it more engaging to follow the sounds of a poem than its sense. Sounds will lead you where you wouldn't otherwise think to go. Frankly, it's easy to make sense. We do it every day. It's more challenging, and more rewarding, to make interesting sounds.

PRACTICE SESSION

1. Write a draft at least twelve lines in length with six true rhymes. All rhymes must be end rhymes. Include a thunderstorm in the draft.

2. Write a draft at least twenty lines in length with six slant rhymes. All rhymes must be internal rhymes. Each rhyming word must appear within two lines of its partner. Include a dog (or a cat) in the draft.

Measured Steps: Meter

On the old television show *American Bandstand*, the host Dick Clark would play a new song and ask a guest to rate it. One time or another, a guest would invariably say, "It has a good beat to dance to. I give it a ninety-eight." The rhythm of poetry works in similar fashion, like a song's beat. English is an accented language, which means we pronounce some syllables with more emphasis than others. They're stressed syllables. (Dictionaries have pronunciation guides that show the stressed and unstressed syllables of a word.) The word *pronunciation*, for example, consists of five syllables: pro-nun-ci-a-tion. Say the word and listen to the emphasis you place on the syllables. The second syllable (*nun*) is a minor stress, the fourth (*a*) is a major stress, and the others are unstressed: pro-NUN-ci-A-tion. Your voice accents the fourth syllable the most.

The rhythm of poetry comes from the interplay between stressed and unstressed syllables. Like the devices of sound, rhythm depends on repetition. It's like the percussion of a song. The bass guitar and drums lay down the beat that tells the dancers how to move. When the beat changes, the dancers respond to that change. That's how rhythm works: The stressed syllables lay down the poem's beat. Listen to the beat Shakespeare uses in Sonnet 73 (the stressed syllables appear in capital letters):

> That TIME of YEAR thou MAYST in ME beHOLD
> When YELlow LEAVES, or NONE, or FEW, do HANG
> UpON those BOUGHS which SHAKE aGAINST the COLD,
> BARE RUin'd CHOIRS where LATE the SWEET BIRDS SANG.
> In ME thou SEE'ST the TWILIGHT of SUCH DAY
> As AFter SUNset FADeth in the WEST,
> Which BY and BY BLACK NIGHT doth TAKE aWAY,
> DEATH'S SECond SELF, that SEALS up ALL in REST.
> In ME thou SEE'ST the GLOWing of SUCH FIRE
> That ON the ASHes of his YOUTH doth LIE,
> As the DEATH-BED whereON it MUST exPIRE,
> ConSUM'D with THAT which IT was NOURish'd BY,

> THIS thou perCEIV'st, which MAKES thy LOVE MORE STRONG,
> To LOVE that WELL which THOU MUST LEAVE ere LONG.

The rhythm of this poem depends on the repetition of stressed and un-stressed syllables in a recognizable pattern. The basic unit of rhythm is the **foot**, which consists of a set number of stressed and unstressed syllables. These feet are not invented, however. They occur naturally in the language, in the way we speak. Poets manipulate them, though, to create the rhythmic patterns of their poems. The **iamb**, the most common rhythmic foot in general and the basic foot of Sonnet 73, is a two-syllable foot, an unstressed syllable followed by a stressed syllable:

> That TIME / of YEAR / thou MAYST / in ME / beHOLD

The first three lines of Sonnet 73 repeat this rhythm exactly (ta-DUM, ta-DUM, ta-DUM, ta-DUM, ta-DUM) and thus establish a pattern of beats, the poem's predominant rhythm.

Too many ta-DUMs in a row, however, grow monotonous, so Shakespeare changes the beat slightly in the fourth line:

> BARE RU- / in'd CHOIRS / where LATE / the SWEET / BIRDS
> SANG.

In both the first and fifth feet of this line, Shakespeare substitutes a **spondee**, a foot consisting of two stressed syllables, for the iamb. A spondee is a double beat (DUM-DUM). In the fifth and sixth lines, he makes other substitutions:

> In ME / thou SEE'ST / the TWI- / LIGHT of / SUCH DAY
> As AF- / ter SUN- / set FAD- / eth in / the WEST,

The fifth line runs iamb, iamb, iamb, **trochee**, spondee. A trochee consists of a stressed syllable followed by an unstressed syllable ("LIGHT of"). The sixth line runs iamb, iamb, iamb, **pyrrhic**, iamb. A pyrrhic consists of two unstressed syllables ("-eth in"). The spondee, trochee and pyrrhic are the natural substitutions that vary the rhythm of a poem.

Two other feet are the **anapest** and **dactyl**. Both are three-syllable feet. The anapest consists of two unstressed syllables followed by a stressed syllable, as in George Gordon, Lord Byron's "The Destruction of Sennacherib":

The AsSYR- / ian came DOWN / like the WOLF / on the FOLD

The dactyl consists of a stressed syllable followed by two unstressed syllables, as in Alfred, Lord Tennyson's "The Charge of the Light Brigade":

CANnon to / RIGHT of them,
CANnon to / LEFT of them,
CANnon in / FRONT of them

The anapest and dactyl are less common meters, but they appear in some of our best loved poems, such as Clement Moore's "A Visit From St. Nicholas": " 'Twas the NIGHT / before CHRIST- / mas, when ALL / through the HOUSE. . . ."

Here, again, are the primary rhythmic feet:

iamb:	ta-DUM
spondee:	DUM-DUM
trochee:	DUM-ta
pyrrhic:	ta-ta
anapest:	ta-ta-DUM
dactyl:	DUM-ta-ta

These feet combine to create **meter**, the recurrence of a rhythmic pattern. We note meter by first naming the predominant foot and then the length of the line; thus Sonnet 73 is written in iambic **pentameter**, a line of five iambic feet. Other common metric lines are **dimeter** (two feet per line), **trimeter** (three feet), **tetrameter** (four feet) and **hexameter** (six feet). All meters allow for an extra unstressed syllable at the end of the line. An iambic pentameter line, for example, may read, "Give NOT / a WIND- / y NIGHT / a RAIN- / y MOR- / row" (from Shakespeare's Sonnet 90). This extra unaccented syllable allows more play in the line and thus lets us avoid some awkward constructions.

The length of the line can set the mood of a poem. Shorter lines—dimeter and trimeter—are sprightly lines, quick off the tongue. They reel off short and snappy. Longer lines—tetrameter and pentameter—are more versatile. They allow greater freedom to substitute rhythmic feet. (Recall the effects Pope achieves in the pentameter lines from *An Essay on Criticism*.) Hexameter tends to be a weighty line, ponderous and serious. Your choice of rhythm and line length depends, of course, on the effects you wish to achieve. Match your subject with lines appropriate to its expression.

One other concern is the **line break**, the end of the line where the verse turns to begin a new line. Line breaks may be **end-stopped** or **enjambed**. Christopher Marlowe's "The Passionate Shepherd to His Love" begins, "Come live with me, and be my love." This is an end-stopped line; it's complete in its grammatical structure and sense. An enjambed line is not complete; it runs on to the next line. The second stanza of John Keats's "Ode on a Grecian Urn" begins, "Heard melodies are sweet, but those unheard . . ." This line must run on to the next line to reach completion: "Heard melodies are sweet, but those unheard / Are sweeter; therefore, ye soft pipes, play on."

Most poems use both end-stopped and enjambed lines. Because the end-stopped line reaches completion, it provides immediate coherence and emphasis. The grammar and sense come together at the line break, and the reader pauses to take in the import of the line. The enjambed line provides momentum and urges the reader on to the next line. There's no pause, but a steady push, deeper into the poem. Each line break is effective in its way. Meter and line breaks work together to slow the reader for emphatic lines or to push the reader onward.

Not all poems are written in meter, nor need they be. In chapter eight we'll look at traditional forms, such as the sonnet, that make use of meter. We'll look at free verse, too, which isn't metric, but establishes its own rhythms. If you're drawn to formal poetry, meter is an indispensable aspect of your poems. You'll find your words slipping naturally into the iamb. From there, you substitute other feet, a trochee at the beginning of a line to set it in motion, or a spondee to emphasize a pair of consecutive words. After a substitution, you return to the iamb, the predominant rhythm. Or you may establish the trochee as your rhythm, or the anapest. Whichever meter works best for the poem, that's the meter that lays down the beat.

 **PRACTICE SESSION**

1. Write a draft in iambic tetrameter, at least twenty lines in length, with one metric substitution per line in at least half the lines. Include

four slant rhymes and the word *Bermuda* in the draft.

2. Write a draft alternating iambic pentameter and iambic trimeter lines. Make metric substitutions only in the pentameter lines. Use the word *down* in the first line and repeat its *o* sound five times within the first five lines. Select a different vowel sound and repeat it five times within the second five lines. Include two similes in the draft.

3. Write a draft in a meter of your choice. All lines except the final line must be enjambed lines. Include two similes and put a lucky gold medallion in the draft.

4. Write a draft in a meter of your choice, with a combination of five true rhymes and five slant rhymes. At least half the lines must be end-stopped lines.

7 ON LOOKING OUT THE WINDOW & LOOKING IN

Edgar Degas, the nineteenth-century French painter, said that one must commit a painting the way one commits a crime. Whenever I'm trying to spark a new poem, looking through my journals for a flash of inspiration, I rediscover Degas's comment, just when I need to be reminded that writing poetry is an act of daring. One must also commit a poem the way one commits a crime. We must be sly and foolhardy. We must forget caution and reason. William Stafford said it well: "Writing is a reckless encounter with whatever comes along."

One year Joan asked for a poem for her birthday. I hid away in my writing room, thought and wrote, slashed out words, thought more. I had several ideas vaguely in mind: that Joan's birthday is on Valentine's Day; that a celebration of one's birth is also a reminder of aging; and that Joan and I have quite different personalities, which is, I think, why we're attracted to one another. Her strengths redeem my weaknesses, and vice versa. After much scribbling, this poem took shape:

JOAN'S BIRTHDAY

14 February

Here's a day, darling,
To dread and love. The snow's
Piled in luscious excess

61

Against the door and the peg-
Legged man's foot-
And peg-prints circle

Round the house. I heard
Him mumbling last night
Outside the window. What

He has to say we'll never
Know unless we listen.
But, darling, he leaves his gift

For you in snow: this marriage
Of flesh and wood. And in air:
The crisp frozen stars

Of breath. Somewhere he's asleep,
Dreaming now of you. Bless him
And his leg, asleep too, dreaming

Of the lathe. And for you, darling,
Happy birthday. Here's
The sun come up, blinding

And everywhere, and here's the snow
Made already less
Than perfect so we can live,

Unlikely companions, with it.

When "Joan's Birthday" appeared in print, I sent a copy to Marylen, my mother-in-law, because Joan is her daughter, but also because I knew Marylen would be quizzical. She'd ask about the peg-legged man. And she did: Who *is* he?

Since the poem takes place on Valentine's Day, I think that he must be some odd manifestation of Cupid. There he is, blessing Joan on her birthday and blessing our marriage, a union of two different kinds of people, a pair of unlikely companions. That's what I told Marylen, any-way. I haven't the faintest idea, really. My peg-legged Cupid, or who-ever he is, simply showed up, tracking across the snow in one of the drafts. I have no idea who he is or where he came from, but he surprised me. I was surprised again by the metaphor "this marriage / Of flesh and wood." My Cupid led me to say things I didn't know I'd say. So he stayed in the poem.

Surprise is important. Robert Frost, in his essay "The Figure a Poem Makes," says, "No surprise for the writer, no surprise for the reader." If the reader knows what's coming, there's no need to read the poem. Readers read to discover. Writers, then, must write to discover. What you don't yet know is more valuable than what you already know. If something or someone unexpectedly shows up in one of your drafts, welcome it or him or her. Make room. Set a place at the poem's table. Perhaps in the end your peg-legged Cupid won't stay in the poem, but your imagination, through its mysterious workings, has offered you a surprise gift, all wrapped up. Turn it around and turn it over. Look at it closely. Shake it to see if it rattles. Let it mystify you. The less sense the gift makes, the better. Precisely because it doesn't make complete sense is reason enough to find out just what sense it does make. Unwrap it.

Remember that poetry isn't saying what you already know. It's discovering what you need to say. Writing poems is asking *what if?* And *what then?* This is an impractical aspect of writing poetry—the sense of wonder and curiosity that can't be taught. You have to develop it. As you write, keep an eye out for the unexpected, the mysterious, the irrational. See what they bring to a draft, but don't explain them away. Each surprise appears for a reason, even if we don't immediately understand that reason.

Poems generate their own ideas and emotions. They take one step, then another, heading into terra incognita. They forge their own paths through the woods, briers and brambles. Follow the path the poem takes, not any preconceived direction you wanted to take. Explore. Look to be surprised. If you follow the poem's path, without knowing where it leads, you'll end up somewhere you've never been before. Your surprise will be the reader's surprise.

In similar fashion, don't stick to facts and truth when they get in the way. Poems are not about *the* truth. Truth changes, depending on what we know. There's always another side to every story. Truth is further complicated because what we know changes every day. And writing poems changes what we know. Poems aren't about truth. They're about exploration. They're about imagination, which we use to understand the everyday complexities and complications. Albert Einstein, one of our premier scientific explorers, said, "Imagination is more important than knowledge." To give your imagination free rein, forget what you know. Forget truth. See where your imagination leads.

Here's a superb poem by Mark Drew, a contemporary poet who ignores a truth in order to explore the emotional complexities of losing a father:

MY FATHER AS HOUDINI

1. *The Car Wreck Challenge*
Pinioned and fluttering,
I breathe gasoline and antifreeze.
I leak blood. My teeth are lost
among the cubes of safety glass
spangling the dash. A crowd gathers.
Where are my assistants? Slender vapor slinks
from the buckled hood, accumulates
about the car and *Poof!*
I'm gone.

2. *The Death Trick*
I'm not supposed to die. No one is.
Everyone wants me to come back;
you want me to come back.
I'm not promising anything,
but think of my body full of preservatives,
think of the shelf life of the soul.
With the right audience, anything is possible
if you just know the trick.
Watch me pull these words from your mouth
like the knotted skein of parti-colored hankies
my mother, your mother, and her mother weep into
at my death.

3. *Metamorphosis*
Larval, straight-jacketed,
my ankles bound and slung from a hook,
I dangle over you like a nightmare and writhe.
Encased in a coffin of water and glass, I squirm,
mouthing secrets so you won't look away.
I'm a ghost shackled in your mouth.
I'm a face hung in a hallway.

I insinuate myself into you.
I've always known how to keep an audience.

4. *The Show Must Go On*
Kid, we live
from deception to deception.
You keep me on stage.
My final trick?
Look at me and I'll live forever;
turn away and we'll both disappear.

I'll say with a fair amount of certainty that Mark Drew isn't the son of Harry Houdini. (The title tells us this: "My Father *as* Houdini.") In place of truth, the poem gives us imagination and an extended metaphor: In a poetic transference, the speaker's father becomes Harry Houdini and tells us of tricks and magic. "*Poof!*" he says, "I'm gone." As part of the extended metaphor, death becomes a magician's trick. In the final section, memory becomes the magician's stage. "Look at me," he says, meaning *remember me*, "and I'll live forever." It's the magic of memory.

If a poem is completely literal, if it's completely true, then the imagination has failed. Really, a poem cannot be completely true. It's a translation of life into language. We each write from a certain subjective perspective. We know only bits and pieces, not the whole. Certainly, we should write honestly about a situation, an event, our reactions to it, our thoughts about it, our emotions. But a poem is a presentation. It's a performance, much like an actor's performance on stage, or a magician's. For truth, readers go to a newspaper. They come to poems for the performance. When you write poetry, let your imagination guide you. Look at the imagery as it appears on the page. Believe in the metaphors. Listen to the sounds the words make. Feel the rhythm of the language flowing across the line. All these aspects of poetry are in play at the same time. At their best, they work together, each contributing to the whole, and thus they create a poem. They're the necessary mechanics of poetry, the craft. But they're nothing without the imagination. Let your imagination guide you, always. Be ready for surprises.

"The practice of writing," William Stafford said, "involves a readiness to accept what emerges, what entices. The sound of words and phrases, the associations of those sounds and syllables in words, the emerging trajectory of thought and feeling." He goes on to say, "A writer coasts into action with willing involvement, always ready for something to happen that may be a first time, not a repetition of something already accomplished."

Say you write on a rainy evening. The rain spatters on your window, a light percussion of raindrops. You have a beginning right in front of you: rain. Does it evoke a mood? Does the rain play a sad melody? Or do you see it brightening the grass and leaves? Does the rain lead you to a memory of another rain—a thunderstorm, a fine mist? What of the events of that earlier day? What simile or metaphor can you derive from the rain? The rain may roll in like a train from the countryside, boxcars loaded with red apples. For each subject that draws your attention, ask *what if?* Put yourself on the other side of the window, on the outside looking in. What do you see—a window lit with the soft glow of a single lamp? What do you feel there, standing in the rain? Or are you walking by the lit window, on your way to—where? Is the lit window a beacon in the storm? Does it mark a safe harbor? Does it warn of a dangerous reef? What if you were above the storm? What if you were waiting for the storm? What if it had just passed?

What then? For every word you write, there are thousands you may write next. Make your poems move and continue to move. Say *another* thing. Every time you reach a *what then*, say several things. An hour after the rain, the water still rushed down the gullies. When the rain stopped, I stood on the porch and listened to the calm. The next morning, the neighbor child placed both hands, fingers spread far apart, into the mud and wondered at the small outlines. *What then?* Where does your imagination lead?

PRACTICE SESSION

1. Write a draft about the best thing before the invention of sliced bread. Begin the draft with a metaphor, include an image of someone's hands at work, and use three slant rhymes.

2. List five important decisions you've made. Consider the effects of each. Select one decision and write a draft with the assumption that you decided otherwise. What is that other decision? What positive effects does it have? What negative effects? Remember, you're not writing

truth. You're inventing. Invent the future that didn't happen. At least three-fourths of the lines must be enjambed lines.

3. Write a draft explaining why the sky is blue. Your explanation must be completely untrue and as convincing as possible. You may invoke ancient Greek gods, the Judeo-Christian God, aliens, a child with crayons, or whatever other explanation you can invent. Include precise images showing how the sky became blue and two instances of synaesthesia.

8 FORMAL GARDENS & WILDFLOWERS:
FORMS & FREE VERSE

When a poem begins to take shape, it tends either toward formal structure or toward improvisation. Poetic forms come with ground rules laid out, the requirements a poem works to meet, the frame it works within. Free verse improvises, making its own ground rules as it goes. Your own personality and aesthetics will lead you to one or the other, but each poem has a mind of its own. One may want to be a sonnet. The next may want to be longer than the sonnet form can contain, or less formally structured. Your poems will assume their own shapes. Each will tell you what it wants to be, formal or free verse.

The Challenges of Formal Verse
Joan has cultivated her flower beds for several years now. Each spring she takes stock of which flowers look best where. She doesn't hesitate to dig up perennials and move them elsewhere. Given the limited space, she strives for perfection in each flower bed: the right number of flowers, combination of colors, depth between the rows, and the right varieties so the beds are in bloom from spring through autumn. My favorite flower bed runs along a white picket fence in our backyard. At each end of this bed, within circles of yellow violas and pink hyacinths, stands a tree—at the right a dogwood with its pink blossoms, at the left a Japanese maple with its scarlet leaves. Joan decided that bright colors would look best against the white fence. Between

the trees she planted lavender daylilies at the back, in front of those are red tulips, in front of those are purple delphiniums, and at the very front are little bells of blue-grape muscaris. It's a formal flower bed, arranged in tiers, balanced from side to side and varied enough that every time I look at it a different color, a different shape, a different flower catches my attention.

Poetic **forms** work with pattern in much the same way Joan's flower beds do. Forms make use of patterns of meter, line length, poem length and **rhyme scheme** (a set pattern of end rhymes). For clarity's sake, when we talk of a rhyme scheme, we assign each rhyme sound a letter. Here's a poem by Elizabeth Barrett Browning, Sonnet 32 from *Sonnets From the Portuguese,* and an outline of its rhyme scheme:

The first time that the sun rose on thine oath	(a)
To love me, I looked forward to the moon	(b)
To slacken all those bonds which seemed too soon	(b)
And quickly tied to make a lasting troth.	(a)
Quick-loving hearts, I thought, may quickly loathe;	(a)
And, looking on myself, I seemed not one	(b)
For such man's love!—more like an out-of-tune	(b)
Worn viol, a good singer would be wroth	(a)
To spoil his song with, and which, snatched in haste,	(c)
Is laid down at the first ill-sounding note.	(d)
I did not wrong myself so, but I placed	(c)
A wrong on *thee.* For perfect strains may float	(d)
'Neath master-hands, from instruments defaced—	(c)
And great souls, at one stroke, may do and dote.	(d)

The letters in parentheses indicate the rhymes, each letter corresponding to a particular rhyme sound. The letter *a* indicates the rhymes of *oath, troth, loathe* and *wroth.* The letter *b* indicates the rhymes that echo *moon.* Discussing the rhyme scheme of this poem, we say it's rhymed *abbaabbacdcdcd.* (Some forms don't require rhyme for every line. In that case, a line that doesn't rhyme is denoted by *x*; for an example, see the ballad form on pages 72–73.)

The predominant meter and line length of Browning's Sonnet 32, and of poetic forms in general, is iambic pentameter: ta-DUM, ta-DUM, ta-DUM, ta-DUM, ta-DUM—ten syllables, five feet of alternating unstressed and stressed syllables. Remember that after you establish the

predominant rhythm, you should occasionally vary the rhythm by substi-
tuting a spondee, trochee or pyrrhic for an iamb. Some substitutions occur
naturally; others are conscious decisions on your part to create emphasis
and metric variety.

The poem's length depends on the form you choose, which means
that it depends on the type and number of **stanzas** the form calls for. A
stanza is a group of lines set apart from other groups of lines by a blank
line or, when a blank line isn't used, by the rhyme scheme. Stanza forms
are determined by their number of lines. (In some poems, especially free
verse, the stanza isn't dictated by such formal concerns, but by units of
thought, like paragraphs in prose; more on this later in the chapter.)
The most common stanza forms are the couplet, tercet and quatrain.

The **couplet** is a rhymed two-line unit, although not necessarily a distinct stanza, as in these lines from Alexander Pope's *The Rape of the
Lock*:

> Not with more Glories, in the Etherial Plain,
> The Sun first rises o'er the purpled Main,
> Than issuing forth, the Rival of his Beams
> Launch'd on the Bosom of the Silver *Thames*.
> Fair Nymphs, and well-drest Youths around her shone,
> But ev'ry Eye was fix'd on her alone.

These couplets aren't distinct stanzas; rather, they're distinguished by
their rhymes: *Plain* and *Main*, *Beams* and *Thames*, and *shone* and
alone. Such couplets are called *rhymed couplets*. In contemporary
poems, the couplet is sometimes used as a distinct stanza form, sometimes rhymed and sometimes not. Unrhymed couplets must appear as
distinct stanzas; otherwise, there's no way to tell they're couplets.

The **tercet** is a three-line stanza, as in these lines from Shelley's "Ode
to the West Wind":

> O wild West Wind, thou breath of Autumn's being,
> Thou from whose unseen presence the leaves dead
> Are driven like ghosts from an enchanter fleeing,
>
> Yellow, and black, and pale, and hectic red,
> Pestilence-stricken multitudes! O Thou
> Who chariotest to their dark wintry bed

The wingèd seeds, where they lie cold and low,
Each like a corpse within its grave, until
Thine azure sister of the Spring shall blow . . .

The tercet originally called for a rhyme scheme of *aaa bbb ccc* and so on.
Poets, however, are always tinkering, creating variations. The stanzas
above are a variation of the tercet called **terza rima**, which interlocks
the rhyme from one stanza to the next: *aba bcb cdc* and so on. A poem
written in terza rima usually ends with a rhymed couplet, picking up
the rhyme of the second line in the preceding stanza: *aba bcb cdc dd*.

The **quatrain** is a four-line stanza, which may be used with a number
of rhyme schemes, including *xaxa*, *aabb*, *abab* and *abba*. Here are the
opening quatrains, rhymed *abab cdcd*, of "Elegy Written in a Country
Churchyard" by Thomas Gray:

The curfew tolls the knell of parting day,
    The lowing herd wind slowly o'er the lea,
The plowman homeward plods his weary way,
    And leaves the world to darkness and to me.

Now fades the glimmering landscape on the sight,
    And all the air a solemn stillness holds,
Save where the beetle wheels his droning flight,
    And drowsy tinklings lull the distant folds.

The quatrain is the most popular stanza form. It allows greater variations of rhyme scheme, and its four lines allow poets to develop complex thoughts and emotions within the space of a single stanza. It offers
room for more play.

Other stanza forms are the **cinquain** (a five-line stanza), **sestet** (six
lines), **septet** (seven lines) and **octave** (eight lines). Some poets have invented stanzas to suit their purposes. The English poet Edmund
Spenser, for example, fashioned a nine-line stanza for his long poem
The Faerie Queene. The first eight lines are written in iambic pentameter, and the ninth in iambic hexameter (six feet); the rhyme scheme is
ababbcbcc. This is the Spenserian stanza, named after its creator.

Play with the stanza forms as you write. Experiment. Try longer and
shorter stanzas. Try different rhyme schemes. Mix them up to see which
stanza most benefits the draft-in-progress.

✎ PRACTICE SESSION

1. Write a draft in iambic pentameter, in rhymed couplets. Use only slant rhymes. Begin the draft with a visual image and follow with an aural image. Include two similes.

2. Write a draft in iambic tetrameter, in quatrains, with the rhyme scheme *abab cdcd efef* and so on. Select ten words at random from the dictionary; use at least five in the draft.

3. Write a draft in terza rima, with both true and slant rhymes. Include a ringing bell in the draft. End the draft with a rhymed couplet.

The Ballad

Stanza forms are the building blocks of poetic forms. The **ballad** is one of the oldest forms. It was originally sung, accompanied by music, to tell stories. It was a part of the oral tradition, before written literature was widely available. It's still primarily a narrative form today. (It's still a musical form today, too, especially in folk and popular music.) The ballad is composed of quatrain stanzas. The first and third lines are written in iambic tetrameter, the second and fourth lines in iambic trimeter. The second and fourth lines rhyme (*xaxa xbxb* and so on), which gives this form its songlike quality. Here's a traditional English ballad (its author is unknown, and in its numerous retellings, more than forty versions of this ballad have sprung up):

THE UNQUIET GRAVE

The wind doth blow today, my love,
   And a few small drops of rain;
I never had but one true-love,
   In cold grave she was lain.

I'll do as much for my true-love
   As any young man may:
I'll sit and mourn all at her grave
   For twelvemonth and a day

The twelvemonth and a day being up
   The dead began to speak:

"Oh who sits weeping at my grave
    And will not let me sleep?"

" 'Tis I, my love, sits on your grave
    And will not let you sleep;
For I crave one kiss of your clay-cold lips
    And that is all I seek."

"You crave one kiss of my clay-cold lips,
    But my breath smells earthy strong;
If you have one kiss of my clay-cold lips
    Your time will not be long.

" 'Tis down in yonder garden green,
    Love, where we used to walk,
The finest flower that ere was seen
    Is withered to a stalk.

"The stalk is withered dry, my love,
    So will our hearts decay;
So make yourself content, my love,
    Till God calls you away."

If you're familiar with the American folk songs about Casey Jones and Tom Dooley, you're already familiar with the ballad form and its ability to tell stories. Its meter and simple rhyme scheme lend easily to song, and the form is versatile: It may have any number of stanzas, however many it takes to tell the story. "The Unquiet Grave" is one of the shorter traditional ballads. Others run twenty, thirty or forty stanzas. The length depends only on the story the ballad tells.

The Sonnet

The **sonnet** is a more concise and regimented form. The term *sonnet* comes from the Italian *sonetto*, "little song." That phrase perfectly describes the form, which is limited to fourteen lines, a "little" poem by most standards. The sonnet was developed in Italy in the thirteenth century. It spread through Europe and arrived in England in the sixteenth century. Through its travels and translations, the sonnet has developed several different forms, all of which, however, call for fourteen lines of iambic pentameter and a sophisticated rhyme scheme.

73

The Italian sonnet (also called the Petrarchan sonnet, after Francesco Petrarch, who along with Dante perfected the form in Italian) is composed of two quatrains (an eight-line unit called the **octave**) and two tercets (a six-line unit called the **sestet**). These stanzas are distinguished by their rhyme scheme rather than by blank lines; the sonnet does not use stanzas, per se, but runs continuously for its fourteen lines. The octave is rhymed *abbaabba*, and it presents the poem's situation, a conflict or challenge. The sestet can be rhymed several ways, *cdccdc, cdcdcd* or *cdecde*. It presents the resolution to the poem's situation. Elizabeth Barrett Browning's Sonnet 32 (on page 69) is an Italian sonnet. Like Browning's sonnet, most are devoted to the subject of love, a convention associated with the sonnet.

The English sonnet (also called the Shakespearean sonnet, after the poet who honed it to its finest achievement in English) is composed of three quatrains and a concluding couplet. It's rhymed *ababcdcdefefgg*. Here's Shakespeare's Sonnet 130:

> My mistress' eyes are nothing like the sun;
> Coral is far more red than her lips' red;
> If snow be white, why then her breasts are dun;
> If hairs be wires, black wires grow on her head.
> I have seen roses damasked, red and white,
> But no such roses see I in her cheeks;
> And in some perfumes is there more delight
> Than in the breath that from my mistress reeks.
> I love to hear her speak; yet well I know
> That music hath a far more pleasing sound.
> I grant I never saw a goddess go:
> My mistress, when she walks, treads on the ground.
> And yet, by heaven, I think my love as rare
> As any she belied with false compare.

Shakespeare puts a twist in the convention of the sonnet as the form of love poems. Frequently, the sonnet idealizes the speaker's loved one as the perfection of beauty, but Sonnet 130 says that this speaker's loved one is far from perfect. In fact, through the three quatrains, it seems she lacks any beauty. The concluding couplet, however, spins the poem around: While the speaker's loved one isn't perfect, she is as beautiful as any woman made perfect through false comparisons. Notice especially the rhyming couplet, *rare* and *compare*, that ends this sonnet. This change in the rhyme scheme from the Italian sonnet to the English—the addition of a rhyming couplet to end the poem—makes for an emphatic ending. It provides a sense of finality. The final word, *compare*, is literally and metaphorically the final word on the subject. The rhyme snaps the poem shut.

The Spenserian sonnet is a combination of the Italian and English sonnet forms. It uses the three quatrains and concluding couplet of the English sonnet, and it interlocks the rhyme scheme from one quatrain to the next, like the Italian sonnet. The Spenserian sonnet is rhymed *ababbcbccdcdee*. Here's Edmund Spenser's Sonnet 79, with modernized spelling:

> Men call you fair, and you do credit it,
> For that yourself you daily such do see:
> But the true fair, that is the gentle wit,
> And virtuous mind, is much more praised of me.
> For all the rest, however fair it be,
> Shall turn to naught and lose that glorious hew:
> But only that is permanent and free
> From frail corruption, that does flesh ensue.
> That is true beauty: that does argue you
> To be divine and born of heavenly seed:
> Derived from that fair Spirit, from whom all true
> And perfect beauty did at first proceed.
> He only fair, and what He fair has made:
> All other fair, like flowers, untimely fades.

The sonnet, in whichever form, is a challenge. It has a demanding metrical structure and sophisticated rhyme scheme. Its brevity calls for precise expression. The finest sonnets, in order to achieve that precise expression, are often highly metaphoric, which generally means the use of an extended metaphor.

While the sonnet is often the form of love poems, it's by no means limited to that subject, as evidenced by e.e. cummings's sonnets "next to of course god america i" and "pity this busy monster, manunkind," poems I recommend to you. Other modern masters of the sonnet form are Edna St. Vincent Millay, W.H. Auden, John Berryman and Robert Lowell. I recommend their sonnets to you also.

The Villanelle

Another form, more complex than the sonnet, is the **villanelle**. It may be written in any meter and with any line length—often iambic pentameter, but iambic tetrameter is common as well. The villanelle consists of five tercets and a quatrain, rhymed *aba aba aba aba aba abaa*. The complexity of the form, however, lies not in its rhyme scheme, but in an intricate pattern of repetition: The first line is repeated as the sixth, twelfth and eighteenth lines, and the third line is repeated as the ninth, fifteenth and nineteenth lines. Repeating lines isn't difficult, but it is difficult to write two lines good enough to be repeated three times each. If the repeated lines aren't good enough, they sound worse with each repetition. Here's a lovely villanelle by Theodore Roethke:

THE WAKING

I wake to sleep, and take my waking slow.
I feel my fate in what I cannot fear.
I learn by going where I have to go.

We think by feeling. What is there to know?
I hear my being dance from ear to ear.
I wake to sleep, and take my waking slow.

Of those so close beside me, which are you?
God bless the Ground! I shall walk softly there,
And learn by going where I have to go.

Light takes the Tree, but who can tell us how?
The lowly worm climbs up a winding stair;
I wake to sleep, and take my waking slow.

Great Nature has another thing to do
To you and me; so take the lively air,
And, lovely, learn by going where to go.

This shaking keeps me steady. I should know.
What falls away is always. And is near.
I wake to sleep, and take my waking slow.
I learn by going where I have to go.

Roethke weaves the repetition in gracefully and repeats lines that are strong and moving. (Notice that he indulges in slight variations in two

of the repeated lines, the ninth and the fifteenth.) The villanelle is a difficult form. It takes expertise to master, but that's the challenge and reward of writing in poetic forms.

Writing in form hones your skills. You must meet the requirements
of the form, which means you write and revise until the poem seems it
can only be a ballad, or sonnet, or villanelle. The lines must flow in their
meter. The rhymes must surprise and yet be perfectly apt. Form is an
artifice in which you try to craft a poem that seems completely natural.
Try your hand at all of these forms. Expect to be challenged. Expect to
be frustrated, and to be elated when a poem masters the form.

Blank Verse

You may also write poems that use formal elements—meter, rhyme
schemes and stanza forms—but not a poetic form, per se. Instead, the poet
writes in quatrains rhymed *abab cdcd* and so on. Or in iambic tetrameter.
Or in **blank verse**, which is unrhymed iambic pentameter. Blank verse isn't
a form, but is a style of formal poetry. Here are the opening lines of
William Wordsworth's *The Prelude*, written in blank verse:

> O there is blessing in this gentle breeze,
> A visitant that, while he fans my cheek,
> Doth seem half-conscious of the joy he brings
> From the green fields, and from yon azure sky.
> Whate'er his mission, the soft breeze can come
> To none more grateful than to me; escaped
> From the vast city, where I long have pined
> A discontented Sojourner—Now free,
> Free as a bird to settle where I will.

Blank verse was the favored poetic line of the theater during the English
Renaissance. Shakespeare used blank verse extensively in his plays and
in his long poems *Venus and Adonis* and *The Rape of Lucrece*. John
Milton wrote *Paradise Lost* in blank verse. Tennyson, Wordsworth,
Keats, Browning and others wrote in blank verse. Its presence is so
strong in the tradition of poetry that it's still widely employed by contemporary poets.

I write in blank verse because I like its formal nature, and the iambic
pentameter line provides structure. It makes me pay close attention to
the words I use and how I use them, their syntax. Because blank verse

provides a strong rhythm, I must decide where to let the rhythm flow and where to vary it. I find myself sounding out words to hear the rhythm, as in these lines that begin a poem of mine called "The Idea of Order":

> BeCAUSE / the WOODS / ROSE THICK / and LUSH / in SUM- / mer,
> TransFORM- / ing E- / ven SUN- / light to / a DARK
> DRIFTing / GREEN, a / PRESence / an AIR- / y BOD- / y,
> BeCAUSE / the FIELDS / ALL LAY / unCUL- / tiVAT- / ed,
> LITtered / with KNIFE- / EDGED GRASS- / es, BROK- / en STONES,
> BeCAUSE / ALL a- / BOUT us / the LAND / GREW WILD . . .

Of the thirty feet in these six lines, only nineteen are iambs, a high degree of variation. (In general, limit substitutions to two per line; otherwise, you lose the predominant rhythm.) Because these lines describe nature overgrown and wild, I freely vary the meter to emphasize the wilderness—content and form working together. The first line establishes the iamb as the predominant rhythm (four iambs bracketing a spondee). The third and sixth lines, especially, vary the rhythm to reflect the wildness of the landscape—three substitutions per line, the meter reflecting the subject. But the rhythm always returns to the iamb. I'm partial to blank verse because it makes me more conscious of the language and the need to craft it.

Blank verse and the other poetic forms make patterns similar to those of a flower bed: repetition and variation. The poet is the gardener, planting the words in the best order, arranging them to provide different colors and shapes, the meters and rhymes of different flowers, growing the poem to catch the reader's eye.

 ## PRACTICE SESSION

1. List the five most intense physical sensations you've experienced. Consider the causes and effects of those sensations. Select one and write a draft in ballad form about it; tell the story of the sensation.

2. Write a draft of a sonnet (your choice of sonnet form). Fashion an extended metaphor to run through the draft.

3. Write a draft in blank verse. At least half the lines must be enjambed lines. Focus on the sounds of the words you select and emphasize alliteration and assonance. Include the names of three small towns.

4. Imitate Theodore Roethke's villanelle "The Waking." Read it several times. Select one of his two repeating lines and use it in the same locations. The other repeating line is up to you. Include a songbird and a bathrobe in the draft.

The Responsibilities of Free Verse

In counterpoint to the formal garden is the field of wildflowers. Around my part of the country, open fields are home to dame's rocket, Queen Anne's lace, bull thistle, fireweed and whitewood aster. While a field of wildflowers lacks the strict arrangement of the formal garden, it's no less stunning. The difference between them is similar to that between poems written in form and those written in **free verse**. Free verse is, simply, nonmetrical poetry. Rather than using meter, free verse makes use of more natural cadences for its rhythm. The stressed syllables of words are still important, but their arrangement in the line is less so. In the same way meter sets up expectations for the rhythm, free verse sets up expectations for the cadences and sounds of the poem. Unlike poems written in meter (which are alike in that they establish a predominant rhythm, vary from it, and always return to it), free-verse poems can vary greatly from one to another. All sonnets, for example, are rhythmically similar, but the same cannot be said for free-verse poems. They don't follow established rhythms. They create their own. Here's a free-verse poem by Ian Clarke, a contemporary poet:

PALE SPRING

Nothing is close in this weather:
A grasp that hushed the world is gone.
Snowflakes lose their spider's touch.

The roads, the frozen troughs between corn rows,
Are not even whitened—onion snow
Like streaked glass over the first ridge of South Mountain.

A crow calls
Where no one has walked.
I turn and face the sound,

Cold as the angel
Who sings over the bronze dead, palming
A flame that gives no heat in either world.

What distinguishes this poem from a formal poem is the absence of a predominant meter. You will notice, however, that it's written in stanzas, the tercet. It makes good sounds: the alliteration of *th* in *nothing* and *weather* in the first line and of *l* in *snowflakes* and *lose* in the third line; the assonance of *o* in *roads* and *frozen* in the fourth line and of *e* in *even* and *whitened* in the fifth line. It makes use of metaphor in the snowflakes' "spider's touch" and of simile in "Cold as the angel." It even makes use of end rhyme in the fourth and fifth lines, *rows* and *snow*, and a slant rhyme in the seventh and eighth, *calls* and *walked*.

You may also notice that the second line is written in perfect iambic tetrameter: "A GRASP / that HUSHED / the WORLD / is GONE." The fourth line is written in iambic pentameter, with a spondee substituted for the iamb in the final foot: "The ROADS, / the FROZ- / en TROUGHS / beTWEEN / CORN ROWS." The ninth line is written in perfect iambic trimeter: "I TURN / and FACE / the SOUND." And the final line is written in perfect iambic pentameter: "A FLAME / that GIVES / no HEAT / in EI- / ther WORLD." Meter may, and often does, appear in free verse, sometimes intentionally, sometimes by chance, but the cadences of free verse are not predominantly metrical. Despite its frequent iambs, "Pale Spring" doesn't create a predominant metric rhythm. Its lines vary in length from three to twelve syllables. Its stressed syllables vary from two in a line to seven. Instead of using meter, the poem paces itself down the page, balancing its phrases in a mixture of long and short lines. It makes use of the iamb, but it moves with the phrase.

Walt Whitman wrote free verse in the 1850s, and the last fifty years have seen free verse become the prevalent poetic style. Free verse began as a rebellion against meter. Beginning in the early years of this century, especially with the poems of William Carlos Williams, free verse has sought to sound more like natural speech—but not, of course, exactly like natural speech. Free-verse poems are as much artistic expressions of the imagination as formal poems are. They still craft language with precision and music. Robert Frost said that writing free verse is like playing tennis with the net down. He favored formal poetry, and his poems reflect that, but free verse is more like racquetball. The ball doesn't pass over a net; it bounces immediately back off the front wall. Sometimes it ricochets off a side wall, or off the ceiling, or flies all the way to the back wall. Some shots bounce short off the front wall, and some bounce long. That's part of the magic and allure of free verse: It creates its own patterns and rhythms. It's free to follow those patterns and rhythms faithfully or to vary from them wildly, thus establishing new patterns and rhythms.

All the elements of poetry are available to free verse: imagery, figures of speech, the devices of sound, rhyme and even meter (as long as meter doesn't provide the primary rhythm). All the stanza forms are available to free verse: the couplet, tercet, quatrain and others. A free-verse poem may make use of several different stanza types, long and short. Or it may make use of sections (with or without titles); see Mark Drew's poem "My Father as Houdini" (on pages 64-65). Here's a free-verse poem by Kathleen Halme, another contemporary poet. It uses both short and long stanzas:

WE GROW ACCUSTOMED TO THE DARK

No one
would know of this.

Two boys idling
an aqua speedboat
did not say no
to the simple question;

we stepped off
the dock and shot down
the black sash of river

past the tourist battleship
and the alligator circus,
past the raw bar's open
ears of oysters,
past the ladyghost in the library,

past five high church spires,
past the cotton shop where
we bought the summer
dresses floating on our bodies,
past her street, Orange, and
past my street, Ann,
past the live oaks dangling Spanish moss,
past the girl under the live oaks
now relieved of the burden
of her virginity,
past the stone wall's fondled holes for cannons,
past the square where slaves in chains were sold,
past the peanut stand and beaded pigeons,
past the scrapyard's parts
of red-brown merchant ships,
past the swampside's hulls of wooden boats,
past the fresh babies, and sound sleepers,
the glubbing clay pipes of plumbing,
and cloth-covered wiring,
past the slack lights
of all the last houses,

down the black sash of river,
back down, all the way to ocean.

There are some ready differences between Halme's poem and Clarke's, as there are between most free-verse poems. The lines of "We Grow Accustomed to the Dark" are generally shorter: The briefest is only two syllables; the longest is ten syllables. "Pale Spring," while it isn't a metrical poem, is more metrical than "We Grow Accustomed to the Dark." Halme's poem follows the cadences of everyday speech, its words arranged much as they would be spoken in conversation, but notice the craft with which those words are arranged. Despite its greater length, "We Grow Accustomed to the Dark" consists of only two sentences. The first prepares us to hear a secret. The long second sentence takes us on a tour, by boat, of a genteel Southern coastal city, giving us a history of the town, its battleship on display, a "ladyghost," the church spires, the old slave market and the old wood-hulled boats.

The main difference between these poems is that "Pale Spring" makes more use of end-stopped lines, while "We Grow Accustomed to the Dark" makes more use of enjambed lines. One kind of line isn't better, or even preferable, to the other. They're just different. The end-stopped lines of "Pale Spring" slow the reader down to linger over the lines. They give the reader pause to consider the sounds and meaning of the lines. The enjambed lines of "We Grow Accustomed to the Dark" push on, leading the reader to the next line and to the next, down the page, guided by the repetition of the word *past*. Past this, past that, down the river, all the way to the ocean.

In these poems, both poets assume the responsibilities of free verse to achieve different results. Free verse isn't exactly free. Clarke and Halme set different rules and goals for their poems. They establish different patterns. Each poem succeeds in its own way—not by ignoring such aspects of poetry as imagery, sound and metaphor, but by creating distinct free-verse forms appropriate for their poems. Free verse isn't complete freedom. It's the opportunity to make your own rules and play by them. That's what poetry is, after all, playing the language to the best effect.

 **PRACTICE SESSION**

1. Select a short paragraph of prose you admire. Rewrite it as free-verse poetry: Write three drafts, each one with different line breaks. Don't repeat any line breaks. Rewrite the prose in drafts of short lines, long lines and a mix of short and long lines. If you find a metric rhythm in the prose, rewrite to emphasize the rhythm.

2. Write a free-verse draft ten lines in length. All lines except the final line must be enjambed lines. Include at least five of the following words: *buzz, careen, dapple, father, maple, muzzle, ravine, steam, stutter, vamoose.*

3. Write a free-verse draft in which all lines are four to eight syllables long. Include your favorite fruit or vegetable in the draft and describe its taste through a simile.

4. Write a free-verse draft in which all lines are eleven to fifteen syllables long. Include an exotic word, two similes, a metaphor and at least four internal rhymes.

AN ASIDE:

9 ON WORK, LUCK & OTHER ACTS OF IMAGINATION

Poems happen one word at a time. There are no shortcuts. The words become lines, the lines become stanzas, and the stanzas become a poem. A good poem, however, is greater than the sum of its parts. The words themselves, each alone, come to nothing. Together, carefully selected, thoughtfully arranged, they engender emotional and intellectual contexts. Images develop that appeal to the reader's senses. Figures of speech create levels of meaning, the literal and the metaphoric. Sounds play off each other in repetitions and echoes. Rhymes chime in, linking important words. The rhythm rolls (sometimes shudders) through the poem. The form of the poem, whether a traditional form or the open playing field of free verse, gives it shape. All these together engender the emotional and intellectual contexts: What happens in the poem affects the reader's heart and mind. This is what poems do at their best. It rarely happens quickly or easily.

Some poets think about a poem for days or weeks before they write the first word. An emotion or idea keeps returning to them. Other poets begin fresh every time, not knowing where the poem will go, but they, too, write on the emotions and ideas that take up residence at the edge of their thoughts. There's the subject, a bone we need to gnaw on, a crooked picture we need to straighten, a garden we need to weed. We may not even know what the subject is until we begin the poem. Then, in the writing, we discover it. We can't help writing about what concerns us any more than we can help thinking about it. If a subject doesn't concern us, it isn't worth writing about. What we feel and think becomes our poems. Not just one poem, either, but five or ten or twenty, however many it takes to fully explore the subject.

We have two tasks, then: to discover our concerns and to discover how to express them as poems. We begin our poems with what keeps returning to us, in whatever ways. Your journal comes in handy for this. Write memories. One memory leads to another, and soon you have an autobiography, the most important moments of your life. Write your dreams, those delightful, irrational, frightening, pleasing manifestations of your subconscious. You needn't analyze your dreams (though you certainly may), but at the very least write the images dreams present to you. Dream images are some of the most vivid and powerful we experience. Write what you see and hear during your day. Listen to people talk. Watch their gestures and expressions. Both speak volumes. Notice their clothing and how they walk. Write your own lines, snippets that may spark the idea of a poem. Write your favorite lines from the poems, stories and essays you read. When you read through your journal later, you'll see patterns emerge, because the writing that affects you as a reader also reflects the concerns that inspire you as a writer.

By all means, read poems. Linger over them. Let them affect you. When you read a poem you love, study it and note your thoughts in your journal. Why do you love it? What does it make you feel? What does it make you think? Look at its images, figures of speech, sounds, rhymes and rhythms. Make note of them, too. A love of writing poetry involves a love of reading poetry. They go hand in hand. One of the first poems I wrote in my journal deals with the love of poetry. It's by Emily Dickinson, "I Dwell in Possibility," (#657):

> I dwell in Possibility—
> A fairer House than Prose—
> More numerous of Windows—
> Superior—for Doors—
>
> Of Chambers as the Cedars—
> Impregnable of Eye—
> And for an Everlasting Roof
> The Gambrels of the Sky—

Of Visitors—the fairest—
For Occupation—This—
The spreading wide my narrow Hands
To gather Paradise—

I love the metaphors this poem presents: Poetry is a house we live in, and writing poems is a way to "gather Paradise." Dickinson is a superb poet to read for metaphors and for the music of poetry, especially in her slant rhymes. Her poems make me think. I feel them. Those responses often begin a poem of my own. Her poems lead me to the words I need to write down.

It's rare that we discover how to express our concerns in the first draft of a poem. The first draft is like a Sunday drive. You go to see where you arrive. You explore the territory and see the sights. You arrive somewhere and know immediately that it's the destination you sought. On a later drive, when you wish to return to that place, then you take the best route. It may not be the quickest route, but the most enjoyable, most scenic, most eventful route. It may take many drives to find the best route. The first draft is that first Sunday drive: You *discover* where the poem is going. In later drafts (there may be many; I wrote forty-three drafts of one poem to get it right), you work on finding the best route. You try a dozen images and keep, perhaps, three or four. You conceive five, ten or twenty figures of speech and keep two or three. You listen to the alliteration and assonance of the words you write and bring in others to compare the echoes and rhymes they make. You set down the rhythm, a good rhythm that makes the ride steady but not monotonous. Or you let the natural (but well-ordered) cadences of your words carry you from start to finish. Then in a later draft, you may find yourself on another Sunday drive, discovering a different destination.

None of this is easy. Nor should it be. A good poem takes time and work. Not every Sunday drive brings you to a place you'll return to, but part of that drive, a seldom-traveled road or two, will be worth returning to on another day, on your way elsewhere. Each first draft is a practice session. You discover something about the craft of poetry, or several things. You discover a subject, or two or three. No time you spend writing is aimless time. Each draft teaches you something. Each gives you something to improve the next time. Like chefs, doctors, baseball players, carpenters and everyone else who practices a craft by doing it, poets practice their craft by writing. The more you write, the more Sunday drives you take, the quicker you discover where you're going, the quicker you discern the best routes. Writing makes you a better writer.

By writing consistently, with daily dedication, you seek out your subjects and hone your skills. You deepen your engagement with the language. You discover and address your concerns. You also allow fortunate mistakes to happen. Just because you didn't intend some word or phrase doesn't mean it isn't valuable. As Robert Frost said, "No surprise for the writer, no surprise for the reader." Let your poems go their own ways. Follow them. Suppose in writing about your first romance, you write the word *sad* instead of *glad*, or vice versa. Suppose you write *homely* instead of *honey*—oops. Calling Dr. Freud! But slips happen. A word comes out dramatically different from what we intended. That's okay. Such a slip may be a fortunate mistake, a stroke of luck. A poem that may have been a ho-hum memory of a first romance takes an unexpected turn. It leads us down a seldom-traveled road to a place we've never been before. Freudian slips are interesting because they seem to get at the heart of things. Sometimes they do. Sometimes they don't. We'll never know if we don't explore the opportunity. Let luck lead you sometimes. Don't be so intent on saying one thing that you fail to say something better. Let go of what you want your poem to say and listen to what it does say.

That's one way of freeing your imagination. Another is to look at your subject from a different point of view. How would your mother and father remember your first illness? What would your first love say about that romance? What does a house builder think of the family that makes the house a home? Imagine other points of view, other characters. You can develop a **persona**, a specific character who speaks the poem. The term *persona* comes from the Latin word meaning "mask." For the sake of the poem, you can put on a mask and craft a **dramatic monologue**, a poem in which the speaker relates a dramatic moment in his or her life. The ballad "The Unquiet Grave" (on pages 72–73) is a dramatic monologue. For a fuller taste of persona and dramatic monologue, read Robert Browning's "My Last Duchess," Robert Frost's "A Servant to Servants" and T.S. Eliot's "The Love Song of J. Alfred Prufrock." You can free your imagination by stepping outside yourself and creating a persona to examine your subject.

You can also free your imagination by selecting words purely for their sounds and then working with their denotations and connotations. If the sound is good, make use of the meaning. You can bring dream images into your poem and treat them as though they're real. You can select twenty words at random from the dictionary and use each in a poem. You can write a poem about going to a place you've never been—and should it be an actual or imagined place? You can imagine an important decision you made and where you'd now be had you chosen otherwise. You can imitate a poem you admire. You can practice metaphors, as in *a teacup of joy*, and make it real: Imagine joy's aroma and taste. Is it served with crumpets? Is it served in the parlor, the garden, the dungeon? And who sips this *teacup of joy* with you? Let your imagination take your poems where it will. It has its own rhymes and reasons, although it may express them slyly.

What if? What then?

"Literature," William Stafford said, "is not a picture of life, but is a separate experience with its own kind of flow and enhancement." Poems are not reproductions of life. They're translations, experience passed through imagination. We make changes to "life" for the sake of the poem. Einstein said that imagination is more important than knowledge. It's more important than minor facts and details, too. Emily Dickinson makes this point in "Tell All the Truth But Tell It Slant" (#1129):

> Tell all the Truth but tell it slant—
> Success in Circuit lies
> Too bright for our infirm Delight
> The Truth's superb surprise
> As Lightning to the Children eased
> With explanation kind
> The Truth must dazzle gradually
> Or every man be blind—

To "tell it slant," we come at truth from a bit off center. Bald truth makes for dull poems, so we circle round it. We come upon it by chance. We discover it. If that means we must alter some fact to discover it, then we alter fact for the sake of the poem. If that means the interstate we drove would better be an oak-shaded country road, then an oak-shaded country road it is. We write what's best for the poem. Don't be so intent on truth that you deny your imagination. In the end, we need be true only to the heart of the matter, the heart of our poems.

 ## PRACTICE SESSION

1. Create a persona and write a draft of a dramatic monologue. The persona may be an actual person or an invented character. At some point in the narrative, whether part of the main action or an incidental event, have a fender bender occur.

2. Choose ten words at random from the dictionary and write a draft using all ten. Title it "Sympathetic Music" and include two instances of synaesthesia.

3. Write a draft based on a dream, but don't announce that it's a dream. Treat the dream as though it actually happened. When in doubt, invent. End the draft with a simile.

10 FROM START TO FINISH:
THE FIRST DRAFT

It's better to begin a poem in wonder than in certainty. It's better to explore and discover. Sometimes, though, in a flash of inspiration, you see a poem in its entirety. Likely it took up residence at the edge of your thoughts, and you've mulled over it subconsciously. That's a way to explore, too, thinking things over without thinking them over. But you must still translate the poem in your head into language. Will it take the shape of a narrative, a meditation, a lyric? Will it consist only of images that evoke your emotions and ideas in the reader's heart and mind? Who are the characters that populate the poem? Where does it happen? What figures of speech encapsulate the emotions and ideas? Form or free verse? You must craft a first line that captures the reader's attention. You must create the tension that draws the reader through the body of the poem. And how will it end? Will it snap shut like a door closing tight, will it end abruptly like a cry suddenly silenced, or will it trail off like a half-spoken sentence that the reader intuitively knows how to complete? For each poem, you make numerous decisions, but you must also recognize the sudden impulses and fortunate mistakes that contribute, despite your best intentions. Now comes the work and play of writing the poem.

What Do You Have in Mind?

Some poems end up being written from the end to the beginning. Others are written from the middle out to the beginning and end. Most start at the beginning and progress to the end. Whichever the case, the poem begins with a first draft and goes through a number of others before reaching its finished, polished incarnation. Days and weeks—sometimes years—may pass before a draft becomes a poem. Rare is the poem that comes out perfectly the first time. Extremely rare. A great deal of thinking and writing goes into even a short poem. In fact, a great deal of thinking and writing goes into starting a poem. Once a poem does get going, it often develops a mind of its own and goes where it will, but before that you start from scratch. A blank page—or a blank computer screen—can be a daunting sight. The trick is to put words down, even if they aren't words that end up in the poem. The trick is simply to write—or to prewrite, the writing that gets the writing going.

You can start a number of ways. You can brainstorm. Make the blank page an idea page. Write down your first idea—a general subject, a statement, an image, a question, whatever. One idea generates a second. The second generates a third. Don't worry about being neat and tidy. Don't worry about being correct and proper. Don't worry about complete sentences. Mess up the page with ideas, one followed by another. Generate as many as you can as quickly as you can—speed is important—and see where your concerns instinctively lead you.

You can engage in freewriting. Give yourself ten minutes and write without pause. It doesn't matter how you start. Write whatever comes into your head, anything at all, everything. Your concerns will manifest themselves because we can't help but write about our concerns. Again, don't worry about complete sentences. Don't worry about logic and making sense. Don't worry about organizing your thoughts. In fact, don't think. Write, write, write. Once you get going, the writing itself will lead you.

You can free-associate, an activity similar to brainstorming, but with the express purpose of jumping from one idea to the next without the benefit of exact logic. Begin with an abstraction, say, *justice*. Close your eyes and what do you see? The image of a blindfolded woman holding a scale? A judge and jury? Henry Fonda in the film *Twelve Angry Men*? A personal memory of justice served or, perhaps, not served? Let one image lead you to another. Write them down, and continue.

You can take a quiet moment, clear your mind and allow an image to come unbidden to you. Hold the image. Concentrate on it and see it clearly. Note the details. Move deeper into the image. Walk through it. What are you approaching? Look from side to side. Turn and walk in another direction. How has the scene changed? Who is there with you? Take a mental picture of the scene. Take an entire roll of film, then develop the pictures on the page. Write down all the details you can, with as much precision as you can.

These are ways to begin, to discover the subjects you'll inevitably write about. One other prewriting activity is to read immediately before writing. I read poems before I begin—not poems I know and love, but new poems in literary magazines. By reading, I put myself in the mood to write and at the same time set my sights. Chances are, I won't like all the poems I read. I may like half of them, but those poems I don't like spur me on to write better poems. By reading, I generate ideas. I respond to poems, whether I like them or not. They start me thinking. I argue with them, and the argument sparks the first draft of a poem.

If you already know what you want to say, you probably don't need to say it. The reader probably doesn't need to read it. A poem that doesn't surprise you won't surprise the reader. It's dull, predictable, the last thing we want for our poems. "A writer," William Stafford said, "isn't so much someone who has something to say as he is someone who has found a process that will bring about new things he would not have thought of if he had not started to say them." Try these prewriting activities. Look back at your journal and see what you've accumulated. Read poems. Admire them and argue with them. When you discover your concerns, when you make sounds that please your ear, when you find intriguing words, begin there, the first draft of a new poem.

 PRACTICE
SESSION

1. On one day, take ten minutes each in the morning, afternoon and evening to brainstorm. Begin each session with a blank page and a new subject.

2. Freewrite for ten minutes per day for five consecutive days. Don't plan ahead. Once you begin writing, do not pause. After the five days, consider which sessions contain the seeds of poems.

3. Free-associate for ten minutes. Begin with one of the following words: *home, pleasure, fast, winter, foul, hollow, river, hectic*. Let each response lead you to the next response. Write quickly. Repeat this exercise as you like.

4. Write a draft arguing with a poem you dislike. At some point in the draft, have the sun shine through an attic window.

In Medias Res and Other Beginnings

In medias res is a Latin phrase meaning "into the middle of the story." A poem beginning in medias res begins in the middle of an event. The situation is already established. The action has already begun. One of my favorite poems, "The Closet" by Bill Knott, begins, "Not long enough after the hospital happened." Such a beginning puts the reader directly in the action, involved in an ongoing situation, and it creates a dual mystery: What happened before, and what happens now? Knott's first line also begs a third question: Who did it happen to?

A good first line of a poem captures the reader's attention and imagination. It presents a sense of mystery, as Knott's first line does, or it makes sounds that interest the reader's ear, or it creates motion—literally, a movement to or away from something—or it notices something new, a fresh sight, perception or idea. The first line also establishes the patterns of the poem, its language, sounds, meter and **tone**. Tone is similar to tone of voice, although in printed poems we don't have the inflection of the spoken voice to reveal tone. Instead, we work with the words and syntax. From Knott's first line, we know the poem is serious, and the repercussions are ongoing: "Not long enough after." We know more time must pass for the wounds to heal, and "The Closet" will tell us about both wound and healing. But not all poems are serious. Tone may be playful, ironic, wry, somber, highfalutin, intimate, slangy, formal, suave or however you want the poem to sound. Tone tells the reader how the poet feels about the subject. "The Closet" is painfully serious. Whitman's "A Boston Ballad" (which in the original version of *Leaves of Grass* begins, "Clear the way there Jonathan!") is boisterous, full of energy, excited. W.H. Auden's "Miss Gee" begins, "Let me tell you a little story," and so establishes an intimacy with the reader, as though the speaker were whispering in the reader's ear.

In his essay "The First Line," Howard Moss, a poet and former poetry editor of *The New Yorker*, notes three types of first lines. The first is a line "which is, in itself, a complete statement"—in other words, an end-stopped line. Three of my favorite end-stopped first lines are Robert Hass's "In the life we lead together every paradise is lost" (from "Against Botticelli"), Kathleen Halme's "With fur and

93

teeth the pushy guests moved in" (from "Something Evermore About to Be") and William Matthews's "It would be good to feel good about yourself for good" (from "Self Help"). Notice that both Hass's and Halme's first lines establish a situation already in progress, in medias res. They draw the reader in to find out the *what*, *how* and *why* of these situations. Matthews's first line begins a meditation, his speaker musing on the nature of self-esteem. Notice the tones. Hass's first line is serious and grand. Halme's is playful, making use of overstatement: The guests are likened to wild animals. Matthews's is playful, too, in a sly way: Why, yes, it would indeed be good to feel good about yourself for good. What these lines share is that each encapsulates the gist of the poem. They announce the subjects.

The second type Moss notes are "first lines in which the second line already holds sway, in which the thing to come is part of the originally given words"—in other words, an enjambed line and the line or lines immediately after. A couple of my favorites are Maxine Kumin's "Blue landing lights make / nail holes in the dark" (from "Our Ground Time Here Will Be Brief") and Pattiann Rogers's "We could sit together in the courtyard / Before the fountain during the next full moon" (from "A Daydream of Light"). Again, these beginnings establish situations already in progress. Kumin's is a literal situation, a plane landing at night. Rogers's is a hypothetical situation, a daydream: "We could." Both make use of strong images, appealing to the reader's senses, and Kumin fashions an intriguing visual metaphor: The lights are "nail holes." The strength of an enjambed first line is that it draws the reader quickly on to the second line. Such a beginning may run to the third and fourth lines as well, however many it takes to complete the first statement. It's two, three or four first lines all wed together.

The third type Moss notes is "not really a first line though it comes at the beginning of the poem." He calls it "a syntactical diving board" that "has no particular interest in itself." Such a beginning is crafted to sound completely casual, an offhand comment, a word in passing, but it's like a door that opens into a surprise party. Such a beginning lulls the reader before the poem springs its surprise. Mark Halliday begins his poem "Population" with such a line: "Isn't it nice that everyone has a grocery list." At first, this seems a nondescript line with its nondescript word *nice*. *Isn't it nice* rings of small talk. But after this understated first line, the poem investigates more heady subjects: lust and loneliness, the need for companionship, our desire for happy endings. Who'd expect such a casual beginning to lead to such complex subjects? Surprise.

The first line sets up the reader's expectations for the poem's language, sounds, meter and tone. It also sets up your own expectations. It sets your goals for the poem, your ambitions. The lines that follow must rise to the quality of the first line. They must be as good, or better. Anything else proves disappointing. As you write a first draft, you may write ten, twenty or thirty lines before you reach the line that actually begins the poem. Those earlier lines may or may not end up in the poem. They may be the prewriting that starts the poem going. What's important is that you recognize the first line when you write it, whenever you write it. It should stand out, the line you've been looking for, the perfect beginning. Your poems need good first lines not only to interest the reader, but also to challenge you to write better lines in the body of the poem.

 **PRACTICE SESSION**

1. Over several days, write twenty to thirty first lines. Don't write the drafts; concentrate on beginnings. By turns, use exotic words, images, figures of speech, devices of sound, internal rhyme and various meters. Experiment with tone. Set the first lines aside for a week, then return to them and select the best five. Save them for future use.

2. Look over your previous drafts. Select the five best final lines. Write five new drafts using those final lines as first lines.

3. Begin a draft of a narrative poem in medias res. Introduce the main characters, one at a time, every three or four lines. End the draft by referring back to the first line.

4. Listen to conversations and note the most casual statements. Select the statement that suggests the most potential. Use it to begin a draft in an offhand manner. Consider the words of that statement and free-associate: What do the words lead you to? Write the draft in a completely casual tone.

Straightaways and Curves

William Carlos Williams called a poem "a machine made of words." Poems must move. Their gears must mesh, belts churn and pistons pump. Strong beginnings and endings are indispensable to a poem, but the lines between them, the middle of the poem, that's where the poem does its work. After you've discovered your subject, written a dozen or more first lines and found the one true first line, now you build the engine of the poem. You build it from scratch. This is the first draft, the prototype, with no guarantee that it will run. That's okay. If it doesn't run, you unbuild it and build another, until you have the first draft revved up and ready to move to the second, third and fourth drafts.

Your first line establishes patterns for the poem, its language, sounds, meter and tone. The question now is whether you stick to those patterns, vary them slightly or vary them a great deal, thus establishing new patterns. The first line also establishes the situation of the poem. Does it suggest a lyric, a meditation, a descriptive passage or a narrative? These possibilities, these options, are all contained in the first line. Now you begin to narrow those options. One of my poems, "Saint Thomas," begins with an enjambed first line, and its opening statement runs to the third line:

> I believe what I can see and taste
> And touch: sunrise, bread, the earth
> Firm beneath my feet.

These lines, taken with the title—"Saint Thomas," the doubting apostle—suggested that the poem explore doubt and belief. I wrote several drafts, trying to discover how to present these concerns, until I decided a narrative would be the best approach. The Testaments, after all, are narratives. The tension of Saint Thomas's narration, too, doubt versus belief, was present in his statement about trusting his senses. Here's how the poem turned out:

SAINT THOMAS

> I believe what I can see and taste
> And touch: sunrise, bread, the earth
> Firm beneath my feet. When I see
> Far ahead Roman spears glinting,
> Approaching, I know the road I travel
> Is their road; the dust, their dust.
> Even from a distance, I hear the rattle

And clank of armor and I know what Rome
And spears can do. In the summer weeds,
Off the road, I stand as they troop by.
When, come to a village, I lift
A cup to my lips, I know the taste
Of clay and of water cool from the well.
As I wash dust from my tongue and face,
I believe in water. When, in the marketplace,
People throng about us, I touch them
And I know something akin to hope
Exists. I hear what they hear and hear
As well the silence between the simple words.
I cannot say what I hear in the silence,
But I hear it, and at night when I lay
Myself down, it follows me into sleep
And I do not dream. There is much
I cannot believe, much that is beyond
My ken, but I have come to know
The silence beyond the reaches of the day.
Come sunrise, I believe in all I can.

This is a persona poem, Saint Thomas expressing his desire to believe, to have faith. The pleasure of writing a persona poem is getting inside the head of a character, seeing what he sees, feeling what he feels. The middle of the poem was engendered in the opening lines, Thomas avowing faith in his senses. The narrative presents instances highlighting each sense, and each instance contributes to the narrative, moving it from the wilderness to a village where Thomas experiences a brief moment of faith and comes to understand that he needs more.

You can think about a poem in several ways: as a house you explore room by room, as a journey taking you from one place to another, as a secret revealed a bit at a time. Or it may be a little of each. "Saint Thomas" is such a combination. The senses are rooms the poem shows us through; we travel literally from one place to another and metaphorically from doubt toward faith; and Thomas reveals a secret: He wants to achieve faith.

"Saint Thomas" went through several drafts before it even began to take shape. A few of its early lines ended up in the poem, but most went into storage. Once the poem began to take shape, it went through several more drafts, each removing weak lines, adding stronger lines and giving the whole more clarity and precision. Each of the images—the Roman troops, the cup of water, the crowded marketplace—took time to develop. Early images were discarded. New images developed. In the early drafts, I never knew exactly where the poem was heading, that in the end Thomas would say, "I believe in all I can." Had I known that as I wrote, the poem wouldn't have a sense of surprise: Thomas's final statement would have been dogmatic rather than revelatory. Instead of leading the poem, I let the poem, and its speaker, lead me.

That's generally how the body of a poem comes to be. In the first lines the poet sees the direction the poem wants to take, then writes too much, then cuts away the excess, the wrong turns, the weaknesses. Then the poet writes too much again. It's like that Sunday drive, going just to see where you arrive. Expect to take wrong turns. Expect both straightaways, where the writing is fast and fevered, and curves, where the writing slows because the road ahead is uncertain. Expect to back-track. Then write more. By writing too much, we give ourselves options. We give ourselves the chance to select the best lines for the poem. Never be satisfied with a first effort. Write more. Write until you have exactly the line the poem needs, or until you discover that the first effort has been the best all along. Give yourself the chance to select lines worthy of the poem, line by line, from beginning to end.

 ## PRACTICE SESSION

1. Select the best and second-best first lines from the previous practice sessions. Use the best as the first line of a draft and the second best as the second line. Write a draft following the patterns these lines together suggest.

2. Write a draft based on a fairy tale. Keep the characters the same, but modify the time, setting and events. For example, you may have Snow White enlisting in the army or Hansel and Gretel at summer camp. Keep old characters you like and introduce new characters as needed.

3. Write a draft about making or building something: an omelet, a V-8 engine, a shed, a quilt, a pyramid, a ship in a bottle—anything you like. Focus on the actions. Some assembly required.

4. Read the outlandish headlines of grocery-store tabloids, but don't read the stories. Select a headline and write a draft telling the story. Invent.

The Final Period

Readers can be kind. They forgive slight missteps in a poem if the ending delights them. The ending, if written with grace, conviction and just the right phrasing, makes the poem a complete experience. It provides the necessary sense of closure, the feeling that the poem has truly ended. A poor ending has the reader turning the page to read the rest of the poem, only to find nothing more. The poem has ended in midcourse and denied the reader a satisfying experience. With a good ending, the reader immediately feels the fulfillment of the poem, an exquisite achievement.

Good endings are as difficult to write as good beginnings. Again, there's no blueprint to follow. Each poem requires something different, depending on how the opening leads to the middle and the middle leads to the ending. But there are types of endings you can adapt and modify for your poem's needs. Maxine Kumin, in her essay "Closing the Door," notes four types of endings. One is a reiteration or repetition of an earlier line. It turns the poem "back on itself, like a serpent with its tail in its mouth," creating a circular movement. The ending appears in the beginning, the beginning in the ending. This type of ending is especially effective with forms—the villanelle form with its recurring repetitions explicitly calls for such an ending—because it allows the poet to reiterate the gist of a poem. Robert Frost was a master of such endings. His poem "Mending Wall," for example, presents the speaker meeting his neighbor at their common property line to rebuild a stone wall. Why rebuild it? The neighbor can say only what his father before him said: "Good fences make good neighbors." The poem deals with following tradition for tradition's sake, for no other rhyme or reason. Frost's speaker can't convince the neighbor that rebuilding the wall is a senseless activity, and the poem ends, "He says again, 'Good fences make good neighbors.'" The final line emphasizes the neighbor's strict, thoughtless adherence to tradition, the absurdity of it.

A second type of ending Kumin describes is "the understatement that startles or arouses." You'll recall from chapter six that understatement creates emphasis because the reader perceives the difference between what is said and what is. The reader recognizes the seemingly unimportant as quite important. Elizabeth Bishop's poem "The Prodigal" presents the squalor of the prodigal son's situation after frittering away his fortune. His plans have gone awry, he drinks too much to ease the disappointment, and for pride he suffers the consequences. He works as a farmhand, living and sleeping in the stink and filth of the animals. He can live better, returning home, if only he will conquer his pride. The poem concludes: "But it took him a long time / finally to make up his mind to go home." In its understated way, this ending accentuates the prodigal son's struggle to admit his failure and humble himself before his father and brothers. His was not an easy decision.

A third type of ending makes "a prophetic or apocalyptic statement." It's a grand revelation, a sweeping statement, and it's a difficult ending to write. The subject and the poem's treatment of it must be weighty, a serious subject deserving a majestic, heightened ending. Kumin calls this ending "a grand clash of cymbals." If the poem doesn't build to such an ending, it's a loud, misplayed note. Sylvia Plath was adept at these endings. Her poem "Lady Lazarus," about an attempted suicide and the pain and anger that led to such an extreme emotional state, ends on a prophetic note: "Out of the ash / I rise with my red hair / And I eat men like air." "Lady Lazarus" makes use of both hyperbole and understatement. It exaggerates and dismisses. It imitates the severe mood swings of deep manic depression. In its final lines, it rises again to the majestic, sweeping statement, "a grand clash of cymbals."

The fourth ending Kumin notes offers "an aggressive shift of balance at the end, closing the door with an unexpected shiver, the shiver of recognition we undergo when the line or lines are apt, however surprising." Such an ending is in perfect keeping with the poem, but it takes a sudden turn, one the reader doesn't see coming. Here's a poem by Walt Whitman that ends on a sudden turn:

ARE YOU THE NEW PERSON DRAWN TOWARD ME?

Are you the new person drawn toward me?
To begin with take warning, I am surely far different from what you
    suppose;

Do you suppose you will find me your ideal?
Do you think it so easy to have me become your lover?
Do you think the friendship of me would be unalloy'd satisfaction?
Do you think I am trusty and faithful?
Do you see no further than this façade, this smooth and tolerant
manner of me?
Do you suppose yourself advancing on real ground toward a real
heroic man?
Have you thought O dreamer that it may be all maya, illusion?

The poem deals with expectations, our best hopes and fondest wishes. Line after line asks about our expectations, then the final line turns suddenly aside to question the expectations themselves. The poem leads us one way, then turns sharply, to our surprise.

As with good openings, good endings often require numerous drafts, each one trying something different. Does the poem end best on an image? Does it end best on a metaphor? Does it end best directly or obliquely? Does it end best by circling back to its beginning or by turning suddenly aside? Then it requires more drafts to phrase it just right. Write several endings, give yourself options, and select the best ending for the poem.

PRACTICE SESSION

1. Write a draft about a small act, such as starting a lawnmower, baiting a hook, pouring a cup of coffee, et cetera. Emphasize each step of the physical activity in precise detail. End the draft by casually mentioning an important moral, political or social concern.

2. Write a draft in the persona of someone famous (actual or fictional) recalling an event from his or her childhood. Recreate that person's voice, or invent an appropriate voice. End the draft with a prophetic statement.

3. Write a draft about a personal experience (return to your important decisions from the practice session in chapter seven). Invent details as needed to create a dramatic monologue. Don't stick to the literal truth. Precede the ending with a simile describing the decision. End the draft with an understatement.

4. Write a draft in which the final line reiterates an earlier line. Include four internal rhymes, four end rhymes and a power tool.

Revision: The Spit and Polish

Taped on the wall above my writing desk is a comic strip, "Non Sequitur," that I clipped from a newspaper. It's a single horizontal frame. On the far left a mob, with upraised fists, torches and pitchforks, urges on a procession of five portly lords, entering from the right, in frilly shirts and powdered wigs, their hands tied behind their backs. One of the portly lords looks back with dismayed countenance. They climb, one after another, a flight of steps to a platform where a guillotine waits with raised blade. Beside it stands an executioner in black hood, his right hand holding the rope that releases the blade. With a droll expression, he tells the lord at the top of the steps, "We prefer to call it editing. . . ."

Editing your poems, revising them, can be a ruthless task, striking out words you labored to put on the page. But it's absolutely necessary. Revision takes three general forms: *immediate revision*, which you do as you write, trying out different words and lines; *spot revision*, in which you revise small sections of a draft, fine-tuning it; and *comprehensive revision*, in which you approach the entire draft, its language, content, structure and focus. After completing a first draft, I spot-revise, tinkering with the poem, making small changes to improve it. After that I wait a week, or two, or a month, before returning for comprehensive revision. The wait is necessary for the passion and thrill of writing the draft to subside. It allows me to gain perspective, to see and understand the draft better. That's what revision is: re-vision, from the Latin *revisere*, "to look back." In revising, we see what's in the draft, what isn't in it, what shouldn't be in it and what should be.

Revision can be ruthless. That's why I wait a while before revising. I need to separate myself from the draft, to forget about owning it. It helps to think of myself not as the writer who put the words on the page, but as a rewriter, someone who finds the draft and says, "I can make this better." That's what revision does—makes the draft better. It makes the draft a poem.

Here are questions and comments to keep in mind as you approach drafts for revision:

- Are the grammar and punctuation proper? If not, do they break the conventions for a purpose?

- Is every word the best word? Does each mean (denote) and suggest (connote) just what it should?
- Is the language mainly concrete-specific? Is the abstract-general language effective, or is it airy and imprecise?
- Are the images as detailed as they need to be? Which contribute to the draft? Which don't?
- Are the figures of speech well crafted and fresh? Do they contribute to the draft, or are they just flashy ornaments?
- What are the draft's most interesting sounds? Are they repeated to create alliteration, assonance and rhyme? Should they be?
- If the draft is written in meter, does the predominant meter create an effective beat? Do the substitute feet—pyrrhic, spondee or trochee—vary the meter for good effect?
- William Butler Yeats said, "Never employ two words that mean the same thing." Is the language as precise and concise as it can be? Which words, phrases or lines can be cut from the draft?
- Avoid archaic diction (*o'er*, *'tis*, *thee*; contemporary writers use contemporary language), archaic inversion (*Upon the cliff I did walk*; use contemporary syntax) and clichés (*white as snow*, *dead in my tracks*, *eyes as deep as pools*; if a phrase comes too easily, be suspicious of it).
- Don't describe the obvious. Which details will the reader understand without them being pointed out? Make use of relevant details; cut the irrelevant.
- Don't explain. The reader takes pleasure in recognizing the relationships the poem suggests.
- Avoid pat emotional descriptions: *trail of tears*, *gentle caress*, *smiling eyes*.
- Avoid ellipses that fill in what's too embarrassing to say. If you wouldn't write the words, don't use ellipses to insinuate them into the poem.
- Avoid unwieldy abstractions: *Time, Life, Truth, Beauty*.
- Treat your subjects honestly (as they are); don't heighten the emotions and ideas to make them appear important. If they're important, the reader will recognize their significance.
- Combine sentences, divide them, extend them or shorten them. A change in the sentence or line can change the tone, even the subject, of a poem.

- Steal from your own poems. Keep all your drafts, even the failures and half-written drafts. They may provide the material for new poems.
- Revise old drafts only if they retain some interest. Look at them occasionally. You may learn from what went wrong or remained undeveloped, and they may provide the phrases, images, metaphors or sounds for the draft you're currently writing.

Because each draft presents different challenges, each calls for different levels of revision. You can revise to sharpen the focus, alter structure, refine theme, remove weak lines, tighten language, improve images and figures of speech, replace an almost-right word with the exactly right word, any or all of these. Finally, look at the poem as a whole and see that everything works together, everything contributing to the whole. Does the opening line draw the reader in? Does the body have the tension and mystery that surprise and delight? Does the ending make a complete and satisfying experience? There's no set number of drafts a poem must go through. Some take dozens, some a few, some only one, and on rare occasion, a poem does emerge perfect. We'd all prefer the perfect poem every time, but we have a responsibility to the poem: If it doesn't emerge perfect, revise, revise, revise. Revise until it is perfect—the perfect poem, the reward.

 ## PRACTICE SESSION

1. Select a draft that interests you. Read it once, aloud, then put it away. Now begin the draft again, from memory. Don't repeat it exactly; write from your memory of the draft. You'll remember its strongest elements, while its weakest fade from memory. Work with the elements that stay with you.

2. Select several drafts you're having trouble with. Which parts are most successful? Put the successful parts of the several drafts together into one draft. Arrange them however you like. Now give the new draft a completely arbitrary title—something like "Before the End" or "After the End"—to see how it changes the draft's subject and focus. Revise this draft of several parts into a new unified draft.

3. Revise a free-verse draft into a form, or a formal draft into free verse. Add a dream and an exotic word to the new draft.

4. Select a rough draft, one you have not yet revised. Rewrite it as prose, with one sentence per line and blank lines between them. Take scissors and cut each sentence from the others. Place the individual sentences into a hat and draw them out, one by one, as the first sentence, the second, and so on. Logic doesn't matter here. Rewrite the newly ordered sentences as lines of poetry, with more enjambed than end-stopped lines. Now begin a fresh revision.

11 REJECTIONS & REWARDS

I've been writing poems for more than half my life now. In 1983 I submitted poems to a magazine for the first time. A couple of months later, the mailman brought me an envelope containing my poems and a small printed slip thanking me for my submissions and offering regrets—my first rejection slip. I'd been warned to expect this, but it ruined my day anyway, and the next day, too. The following years brought me more rejection slips, some with handwritten notes. Then in the autumn of 1987, the mailman brought me an envelope with a letter from the editor of a small magazine. He wanted to publish one of my poems. I was ecstatic. The magazine came out, and there was my first published poem. Surely, this was the first of hundreds, thousands, the beginning of a new era. I wrote poems, rewrote and submitted them. The envelopes returned bearing sad tidings, more rejections. It would be three more years before another of my poems appeared in a magazine. Rejection, too, is part of the process. "An editor," William Stafford said, "is a friend who helps keep a writer from publishing what should not be published." Editors save the poet the embarrassment of publishing bad poems. While rejection is disappointing, it's a challenge to write better poems. That's what this odd venture is all about. Publication is recognition, and yes, it feels good, but it isn't the reward for writing. The reward lies in the small, perfect shape of a poem, the words you put together to say what only you can say, an artistic expression of your imagination, written with precision and grace.

If you choose to submit your poems to magazines, you need to abide by the necessities and courtesies of the writer-editor relationship. Know the magazine you wish to submit poems to. Check your library and bookstores to discover literary magazines, and check such sources as *Poet's Market* to discover magazines you can't find locally. Subscribe to four or five of these magazines and read them thoroughly and critically. (If you don't care for a magazine, allow your subscription to lapse and subscribe to another.) Understand the editors' tastes and preferences. Some editors are more insightful than others. Make sure your poems are appropriate for a particular magazine. If your poems aren't appropriate for an editor, it's a waste of time, ink and postage to submit your poems to that magazine. Make sure you like the poems printed in that magazine. If you don't appreciate an editor's tastes, don't submit to that magazine. You certainly don't want your poem appearing next to poems you dislike.

Once you discover appropriate magazines, look for their addresses and submission guidelines, printed in their first few pages. Proofread your poems with care. Ensure they're proper and correct, free of errors. Send only clean copies, three or four poems at a time. If a poem is smudged or creased so seriously that it's ready to split in two, make fresh copies. Editors appreciate clean manuscripts; they make for a more pleasurable reading experience. Most editors enjoy a cover letter preceding the poems. A simple *hello* will do: Hello, please consider these poems, thank you. If you wish, you may briefly introduce yourself. You may compliment a poem or two in a recent issue (but don't overdo it; editors recognize insincerity). Always address the cover letter to a specific editor, by name. This is a social grace, and it shows that you're familiar with the magazine. Editors appreciate that. With every submission, include a self-addressed, stamped envelope (a SASE) for the editor's response to your poems. Magazines work on tight budgets; they can't afford to respond if you don't send a SASE. You won't hear back, and your poems will hang in limbo. Finally, wait patiently for the editor's response. Magazines receive thousands of poems each year, and sometimes editors get behind. Wait patiently because they have plenty of reading and only so many hours in a day. If you don't hear back within three or four months (check the magazine's guidelines for its response time), write a letter asking if your poems arrived, and if they did, whether they are still under consideration. Send a SASE with a letter of inquiry, too.

When you submit, be prepared to receive a rejection slip. It isn't personal. It isn't a comment on your poems. Editors receive more poems than they can possibly publish. The load is staggering. At *The Gettysburg Review*, we received eight-thousand-plus poems a year. We couldn't even publish all the poems we liked because we had only so many pages to work with. We could accept roughly eighty or so poems a year for publication. We returned many good poems, with our regrets, to their authors. When we had time while reading our eight-thousand-plus poems, we wrote a personal note. Sometimes we offered to read more of a poet's work. When you receive such a note, don't immediately submit just any batch of poems. Many poets make that mistake. Instead, go through your poems, read them with a discerning eye, and send better poems than those just returned to you. If you don't have better poems ready to submit, wait. Write more poems, better poems. Keep the editor's note—and name—so you can send the better poems when they're ready. Take up such an offer only when you can send better poems. Don't deluge an editor with mediocre poems; you want to establish a professional relationship. You want the editor to take an interest in your work. If you send lesser poems, that interest quickly ebbs. Be discerning, make good judgments, develop professional relationships, and you'll see your poems into print.

Keep in mind, though, what Denise Levertov said, "The poet does not *use* poetry, but is at the service of poetry." We cannot finally know the value of our own poems. We cannot even gauge accurately who the best poets of our time are. Future generations will make that judgment. Then generations after them will judge again. William Stafford offered this bit of advice: "What one has written is not to be defended or valued, but abandoned: Others must decide significance and value." What we have is the work and pleasure of writing and, finally, the responsibility. Our responsibility is simple: to write the best poems we can. We write because we have to, the urge to create pushing us on. We make art of what we do.

All terms appearing in bold type in the text and index of this book are defined in this glossary.

abstract term: a word representing an idea or quality that is conceptual rather than tactile; *pride,* *honor,* *love* and *beauty* are abstract terms. Contrast with **concrete term.**

alliteration: the repetition of identical consonant sounds: "*S*he *s*carce could *s*ee the *s*un" (from "The Blessed Damozel" by Dante Gabriel Rossetti).

anapest: a metrical **foot** consisting of three syllables—two unstressed syllables followed by a stressed syllable (ta-ta-DUM).

apocopated rhyme: a type of **slant rhyme** in which **true rhyme** sounds fall on a stressed and then an unstressed syllable: *bow* (BOW) and *fallow* (FALlow).

assonance: the repetition of identical vowel sounds: "But, *a*s he w*a*lked, King *A*rthur p*a*nted h*a*rd" (from "Idylls of the King" by Alfred, Lord Tennyson).

ballad: a poetic **form,** originally sung; the ballad stanza is written in alternating lines of **iambic tetrameter** (first and third lines) and iambic **trimeter** (second and fourth lines). The second and fourth lines rhyme. The ballad is primarily a narrative form.

blank verse: unrhymed **iambic pentameter.**

cacophony: a combination of harsh sounds that grate on the ear. Contrast with **euphony.**

cinquain: a five-line **stanza.**

concrete term: a word describing a quality that appeals to one or more of the senses: *cold,* *hot,* *soft,* *hard,* *bland* and *spicy* are concrete adjectives; *book,* *table* and *car* are concrete nouns. Contrast with **abstract term.**

connotation: the emotional and intellectual suggestions a word carries in addition to its **denotation.**

consonance: the repetition of similar consonant sounds in words with dissimilar vowel sounds: *beard* and *board.*

couplet: a **stanza** of two lines. Originally, couplets were rhymed and their grammatical structure and idea complete within the two lines.

dactyl: a metrical **foot** consisting of three syllables—a stressed syllable followed by two unstressed syllables (DUM-ta-ta).

denotation: the dictionary definition of a word. Also see **connotation**.

dimeter: a line of poetry consisting of two feet. See **meter**.

dramatic monologue: a poem in which the speaker, often a **persona**, relates a dramatic moment in his or her life. The dramatic monologue is primarily narrative.

end rhyme: **rhyme** occurring at the end of two or more lines.

end-stopped line: a line of poetry in which both the grammatical structure and the sense are complete. "Come live with me and be my love" (from "The Passionate Shepherd to His Love" by Christopher Marlowe) is an end-stopped line, complete in both its grammatical structure and sense. Contrast with **enjambed line**.

enjambed line: a line of poetry in which the grammatical structure and the sense are not complete but continued in the following line. "Heard melodies are sweet, but those unheard" is an enjambed line; the following line is "Are sweeter; therefore, ye soft pipes, play on" (from "Ode on a Grecian Urn" by John Keats). Contrast with **end-stopped line**.

euphony: a combination of sounds that please the ear. Contrast with **cacophony**.

extended metaphor: a sequence of **metaphors**, based on a single association, that runs throughout a poem. Such a metaphor is highly developed and consistent in its application of associations.

feminine rhyme: **rhyme** occurring in words of two or more syllables in which the concluding syllables are unstressed: *reason* (REASon) and *season* (SEASon). Also see **masculine rhyme**.

figure of speech: a type of rhetoric used to achieve special effects. See **metaphor, metonymy, overstatement, paradox, simile, synaesthesia, synecdoche** and **understatement**.

foot: a unit of **meter** consisting of a set number of stressed and/or unstressed syllables. See **meter**.

form: a pattern of **meter**, line length, poem length and **rhyme scheme**. Some common forms are the **ballad, sonnet** and **villanelle**.

free verse: non-metrical poetry. Rather than using **meter**, free verse makes use of natural cadences for its rhythm. Meter may be used in free verse, but the rhythms of free verse are not predominantly metrical.

general term: a word signifying a broad class of persons, things or actions. Contrast with **specific term**.

hexameter: a line of poetry consisting of six feet. See **meter**.

iamb: a metrical **foot** consisting of two syllables—an unstressed syllable followed by a stressed syllable (ta-DUM). The iamb is the most common metrical foot in English poetry.

imagery: a word or phrase that presents sensory detail for the reader to experience. Images appeal to one or more of the five senses: sight, smell, touch, hearing and taste.

internal rhyme: rhyme occurring in the middle of one or more lines.

line break: the end of a line of poetry. See **end-stopped line** and **enjambed line**.

masculine rhyme: rhyme occurring in single-syllable words, as in *can* and *pan*, or in the stressed, concluding syllables of words, as in *align* (aLIGN) and *refine* (reFINE). Also see **feminine rhyme**.

metaphor: a **figure of speech** that implicitly equates one thing with another, with the first thing assuming the characteristics of the second. "Sometime too hot the eye of heaven shines" (from Sonnet 18 by William Shakespeare) contains a metaphor equating the sun with "the eye of heaven."

meter: the recurrence of a rhythmic pattern in which stressed and unstressed syllables are repeated. The basic rhythmic unit is the foot. The common feet are the **iamb, trochee, spondee, pyrrhic, anapest** and **dactyl**. The common metric lines are **dimeter** (two feet), **trimeter** (three feet), **tetrameter** (four feet), **pentameter** (five feet) and **hexameter** (six feet).

metonymy: a **figure of speech** in which the name of one thing is substituted for that of another. Metonymy occurs when "the White House" is used to refer to the President and "the crown" to refer to a king or queen.

mixed metaphor: a **metaphor** in which the elements are incongruous, as in "He boiled with joy and she bubbled with anger." The incongruity here is that the verbs and their respective emotions don't coincide: Metaphorically, joy bubbles and anger boils.

octave: the first eight lines of an Italian **sonnet**. The octave develops the situation of the poem, which is then resolved in the **sestet**.

onomatopoeia: the use of words that imitate sounds and suggest their meaning, such as *buzz, crack, hiss, murmur, sizzle, snap* and *whirr*.

overstatement: a **figure of speech** in which exaggeration is used for emphasis or humor. Contrast with **understatement**.

paradox: a figure of speech in which a statement seems contradictory, but is nonetheless true. When Juliet, in Shakespeare's play *Romeo* *and Juliet,* bids goodnight to Romeo by saying, "Parting is such sweet sorrow," she employs paradox. Their parting is sorrowful, but it's also sweet because they look forward to their next meeting.

pentameter: a line of poetry consisting of five feet. See **meter.**

persona: the term *persona,* from the Latin, means "mask." A persona is a character created to speak a first-person poem; it is an *I* who can be distinguished from the author. Also see **dramatic monologue.**

pyrrhic: a metrical **foot** consisting of two syllables, both unstressed (ta-ta).

quatrain: a **stanza** of four lines. Quatrains may be unrhymed or they may accommodate a number of **rhyme schemes,** the most common of which are *abab, aabb* and *abba.*

repetition: a rhetorical device that repeats a word or phrase or reiterates an idea.

rhyme: the repetition of identical vowel and consonant sounds, such as al*one,* b*one* and c*one* (**true rhyme**). Rhyme may also be the repetition of similar but not identical vowel and consonant sounds, as in b*ent* and p*ant* (**slant rhyme**). Also see **apocopated rhyme, end rhyme, internal rhyme, masculine rhyme** and **feminine rhyme.**

rhyme scheme: a consistent pattern of **rhyme** in a **stanza** or poem, as in the English **sonnet,** which rhymes *ababcdcdefefgg.*

septet: a **stanza** of seven lines.

sestet: the final six lines of an Italian **sonnet.** The sestet provides a resolution to the situation developed in the **octave.**

simile: a **figure of speech** that explicitly compares one thing to another through the words *like* or *as.* "O my Luve's like a red, red rose" (from "A Red, Red Rose" by Robert Burns) is a simile comparing the speaker's "Luve" to a rose.

slant rhyme: an imperfect **rhyme** in which **alliteration, assonance** or **consonance** are substituted for **true rhyme.** Examples of slant rhyme are *love* and *give* (slant rhyme using alliteration), *lake* and *fate* (slant rhyme using assonance) and *speak* and *spook* (slant rhyme using consonance).

sonnet: a poetic form consisting of fourteen **iambic pentameter** lines and following one of several **rhyme schemes.** The Italian sonnet rhymes *abbaabbacdecde* (or *cdccdc, cdcdcd*). The English sonnet rhymes *ababcdcdefefgg.* The Spenserian sonnet rhymes *ababbcbccdcdee.*

speaker: the voice (or character) that "speaks" the poem. Also see **persona.** The speaker is not necessarily the poet.

specific term: a word referring to an individual type of a larger group: *maple* and *oak* are specific terms; *tree* is a **general term.** Contrast with **general term.**

spondee: a metrical **foot** consisting of two syllables, both strongly stressed (DUM-DUM).

stanza: a group of lines set apart from other groups of lines by blank lines. Stanzas are often determined by length, metrical structure and **rhyme scheme.** In some poems, the stanza is dictated by units of thought rather than formal concerns. Common stanzas are the **couplet, tercet** and **quatrain.**

synaesthesia: a **figure of speech** in which something perceived by one sense is described in the terms of another sense. Synaesthesia occurs in the image "the creaking empty light" (from "Aubade" by Edith Sitwell). While light is perceived through the sense of sight, here it's described in terms of hearing.

synecdoche: a **figure of speech** in which a part represents the whole or the whole represents a part. Synecdoche occurs when "wheels" is used to refer to a car (a part representing the whole) and when "the law" is used to refer to a police officer (the whole representing a part).

tercet: a **stanza** of three lines. Originally, the lines of a tercet stanza ended with the same rhyme. Also see **terza rima.**

terza rima: a **tercet** that interlocks the rhyme from one stanza to the next: *aba bcb cdc,* and so on.

tetrameter: a line of poetry consisting of four feet. See **meter.**

tone: similar to tone of voice, tone reveals the poet's attitudes toward the poem's subject. Tone may be playful, ironic, wry, somber, highfalutin, intimate, slangy, formal, suave or any of numerous other attitudes.

trimeter: a line of poetry consisting of three feet. See **meter.**

trochee: a metrical **foot** consisting of two syllables—a stressed syllable followed by an unstressed syllable (DUM-ta).

true rhyme: the repetition of identical vowel and consonant sounds. In words of multiple syllables, the rhyme appears in the stressed syllables, as in *avow* (aVOW) and *allow* (alLOW). See **rhyme.**

understatement: a **figure of speech** in which something is presented as less than it actually is. Understatement creates emphasis through the

113

reader's recognition of the difference between what is said and what is. Contrast with **overstatement**.

villanelle: a complex poetic form of nineteen lines, generally **iambic pentameter**. It consists of five **tercets** and a **quatrain**, rhymed *aba aba aba aba aba abaa*. In addition to its **rhyme scheme**, the villanelle makes use of an intricate pattern of repetition: The first line is repeated as the six, twelfth and eighteenth lines; the third line is repeated as the ninth, fifteenth and nineteenth lines.

INDEX

115